D1474816

# Selected Poems of Amy Lowell

# SELECTED POEMS OF AMY LOWELL

EDITED BY

MELISSA BRADSHAW

AND ADRIENNE MUNICH

RUTGERS UNIVERSITY PRESS

NEW BRUNSWICK, NEW JERSEY, AND LONDON

Library of Congress Cataloging-in-Publication Data

Lowell, Amy, 1874–1925.
  [Poems. Selections]
  Selected poems of Amy Lowell / edited by Melissa Bradshaw and Adrienne Munich.
      p.  cm.
  ISBN 0-8135-3127-6 (cloth :  alk. paper)—ISBN 0-8135-3128-4 (pbk.: alk. paper)
  I. Bradshaw, Melissa, 1969–   II. Munich, Adrienne.   III. Title.

PS3523.O88 A6 2002
811'.52—dc21                                                                    2002023715

British Cataloging-in-Publication information is available from the British Library.

Manufactured in the United States of America

*For Rachel and Olivia*

# CONTENTS

## II. CADENCED VERSE

# ACKNOWLEDGMENTS AND PERMISSIONS

It gives us great pleasure to acknowledge the Trustees under the will of Amy Lowell, who have given us permission to reprint the poems under copyright; publication from letters by Amy Lowell and William Rose Benét is by permission of the Houghton Library, Harvard University. Our thanks also go to the libraries at the State University of New York at Stony Brook and New York University, the Houghton Library at Harvard University, and the New York Public Library; to the descendants of Amy Lowell—Gaspard D'Andelot Belin, Harriet Lowell Bundy Belin, and Michael Putnam—for selecting a favorite poem; and to our colleagues, Paul Dolan, Eric Haralson, Peter Manning, and Susan Schekel for rendering opinions and advice. We are grateful for friends and family who reviewed our work and our judgments: Chris Froula, Natalie Gerber, Jaime Harker, Matt Henning, Michael Holko, Rachel Jacoff, Clare Logan, Matthew Munich, Richard Munich, Michael Putnam, Pat Spacks, and Maura Spiegel. We thank the reader for the Press, Camille Roman, and Leslie Mitchner, our great and constant editor. Rachel Poulsen helped at every stage. Olivia Bronzo Munich will hear these poems recited until she is able to read them herself.

## A NOTE ON THE TEXT

The poems in this edition have been taken from the earliest published versions that we could find, for the most part from contemporary periodicals and poetry anthologies. We print them in the versions in which they were originally published, although we have silently corrected the spelling of geographical locations when Lowell herself made those corrections in her published volumes. Except when noted, we retain the spelling and punctuation of the originals.

# "LET US SHOUT IT LUSTILY": AMY LOWELL'S CAREER IN CONTEXT

*Melissa Bradshaw*

> The life of a poet is . . . a mixture of that of a day-laborer,
> a traveling salesman, and an itinerant actress.
>
> —*Amy Lowell, letter to Carlotta Lowell, July 18, 1919*

A T THE TIME of her sudden death in 1925 Amy Lowell was, arguably, the most powerful woman in American poetry. Certainly she was the most well known. Within a period of thirteen years, beginning with the publication of her first volume of poetry in 1912 and lasting until her death thirteen years later at age fifty-one, she produced six volumes of poetry, two volumes of criticism, a two-volume biography of John Keats, and countless articles and reviews. During this time she also toured the country tirelessly, giving lectures and readings, promoting poetry with a fervor that led T. S. Eliot to dub her the "demon saleswoman."[1] At the height of her popularity Lowell's books (both her poetry and her criticism) topped best-seller lists, with first printings usually selling out during prepublication advance sales and going into second and third printings almost immediately. Three more volumes of poetry were published posthumously, the first of which, *What's O'Clock*, won the 1926 Pulitzer Prize. At her death, a memorial tribute in the *Literary Digest* called her a "modern of the moderns," and described her power in the "principality of modern poetry" as "almost autocratic."[2]

In the nearly three-quarters of a century since her death, how-
ever, the woman of whom Louis Untermeyer once said "no poet
living in America has been more fought for, fought against and
generally fought about" has become little more than a footnote to
discussions of more canonical modern poets like H.D. (Hilda Doo-
little), Robert Frost, and Ezra Pound.[3] Memoirs of her contempo-
raries, as well as biographies and even critical evaluations, focus
less on her work than they do on her public persona and, more
specifically, on her body, which, at a height of five feet and a weight
of two hundred pounds, sparked countless cruel witticisms at her
expense, such as Witter Bynner's name for her, "the Hippopoet-
ess."[4] Indeed, Lowell's weight and her feud with Ezra Pound have
proved until recently to be her most enduring legacy. The Amy
Lowell who survives today is more often than not characterized as
a wealthy, headstrong, literary impresario rather than a poet in her
own right, a self-indulgent, self-promoting autocrat.

Anecdotes, rumors, and legends surround Lowell's memory:
smoking cigars; arriving chronically late, even to meet her own
guests; delighting in grand entrances; writing all night and sleep-
ing all day; and, perhaps most notoriously, openly cohabitating
with Ada Dwyer Russell, a former actress and a divorcée. Amy Lo-
well appears in remembrances as an heiress, spinster, lesbian, or-
ator, conservative, patron of impoverished poets, crusader for the
new poetry, the first female Lowell to ever speak in public, and, in
her own words, "the last of the barons." As reporter Elizabeth Shep-
ley Sergeant has observed, "she could not help arousing sensation
wherever she went—love or hate, curiosity, suspense, drama. She
lived dramatically, opulently, always for spectators."[5] She thrived
on publicity and pomp, behaving with a sense of entitlement and
infallibility born of belonging to one of Boston's oldest and most
prominent families.

Born in February of 1874, the youngest of Augustus and Kath-
erine Lowell's five children, Amy Lowell inherited a name synony-
mous with power and wealth. The Lowells dominated industry
and the arts in Massachusetts from the arrival of the first family
member, a British merchant named Percival Lowle, in 1639. The
men of her lineage were the politicians, industrialists, clergymen,

bankers, and academics who built Massachusetts. She also inherited the Lowell disposition: S. Foster Damon, Lowell's first biographer, describes the Lowells as men who were "astonishingly indifferent to the opinions of others, [and] who were much given to public benefactions and controversies."[6]

Lowell started writing poetry at the relatively late age of twenty-eight. Once she decided to make a career of poetry, she spent the next ten years slowly and methodically training herself, since, like most young women of her class and social position, her formal education was limited and did not extend much beyond that provided by private tutors. At thirty-eight she published her first volume of poetry, A Dome of Many-Coloured Glass (1912). Shortly after its publication, she read the poems of one H.D. Imagiste in a 1913 issue of Harriet Monroe's magazine Poetry. The imagists, a small, loosely joined group of poets, aligned themselves against what Ezra Pound termed the "morbid romantic attitude and outworn false generalities" of nineteenth-century poetry.[7] These artists strove for a new form of poetic expression, one that stressed "simplicity and directness of speech; subtlety and beauty of rhythms; . . . clearness and vividness of presentation; and concentration."[8]

Amy Lowell recognized in imagism some of the techniques she herself was trying to perfect. Later that year she traveled to England to meet the poets writing under this banner: H.D., Richard Aldington, and Ezra Pound. Enthusiastic about their work and eager to join their movement, she shared her poetry with them. Pound included one of her poems in his 1914 anthology Des Imagistes, but by the next year he had moved on to vorticism, disowning the imagist movement, which he claimed had deteriorated into overly sentimental "Amygism." Lowell, undeterred by Pound's disapproval, determined to bring the struggling poets she had met in England to the American public's attention. For three consecutive years—1915, 1916, and 1917—she edited Some Imagist Poets, an anthology featuring poems by Aldington, H.D., John Gould Fletcher, F. S. Flint, D. H. Lawrence, and herself. The variety of poetic styles represented in the anthology reflects the elasticity of imagism, which, Lowell explained countless times, "refers more to the manner of presentation than to the thing presented," and places highest importance on "a clear presentation of whatever the author wishes to convey."[9] At the same time she began her campaign to educate the American public—through articles, reviews, and lectures—about the "New Poetry." While Lowell's first book was neither a critical nor commercial success, her next book, *Sword Blades and Poppy Seed* (1914), garnered both critical acclaim and public enthusiasm. The publication of this book established her status as a best-selling poet, as well as a popular lecturer and respected authority on modern poetry. But more than that, this volume, and Lowell's accompanying promotional campaign, transformed her into an American celebrity.

To be sure, she had the advantage of being in the right place at the right time. The year Lowell's first volume was published, 1912, marked the beginning of a poetry renaissance in American popular culture. Also publishing first volumes of poetry that year were fellow New Englanders Robert Frost and Edna St. Vincent Millay, while in Chicago, Harriet Monroe began the revolutionary *Poetry: A Magazine of Verse*. The centrality of poetry in popular culture during these years might be hard for contemporary readers to imagine, particularly because most current narratives of modernist art insist on its lack of public support. In fact, audiences flocked to poetry readings and bought unprecedented numbers of volumes during this period because they were actively courted. While Eliot would later contend that reading poetry requires knowledge, training, and powers of concentration available only to a select few, Monroe believed the general public would respond to unusual, creative, challenging poetry. In an announcement soliciting material from contemporary poets she promised that "while the ordinary magazines must minister to a large public little interested in poetry, this magazine will appeal to, and it may be hoped will develop, a public primarily interested in poetry as an art, as the highest, most complete human expression of truth and beauty."[10] She underscored this commitment to developing an audience of avid poetry readers in her choice of a quote by Walt Whitman for the magazine's masthead: "To have great poets there must be great audiences too."

From the beginning of her career, Amy Lowell's poetry readings captivated audiences. The term *readings,* however, does not adequately describe the way she presented her poems: these were theatrical events. In her first public reading, for example, she arranged to have her friend, the composer Carl Engel, stand behind a curtain and simulate the sound of bombs dropping by beating on a bass drum as she read a series of war poems.[11] Coached by Russell, who retired from a successful stage career in order to move in with Lowell, she worked to exploit the dramatic potential of her poems. Russell taught her how to integrate stage techniques into her readings: she learned how to manipulate her tempo, tone, and volume, moving between shouts and whispers, periods of frenzied, accelerated recitation, and long moments of complete silence; she added hand and facial gestures for emphasis, stamped her foot in time to the poems' rhythms, and even threw in a few dance steps, such as the cakewalk.

Her theatricality, along with the forcefulness of her sweeping pronouncements about the state of contemporary poetry, earned her a devoted, almost cult following of fans who mobbed train stations to get her autograph (thus necessitating police escorts) and who packed auditoriums to standing-room-only capacity in order to hear her speak. Poet John Brooks Wheelwright joked that she was "the Biggest Traveling One-Man Show since Buffalo Bill caught the Midnight Flyer to Contact Mark Twain," and Van Wyck Brooks wrote, "she whizzed and she whirred, and she rustled and rumbled, and she glistened and sparkled and blazed and blared." Louis Untermeyer insisted that she was not merely a lecturer, but "an event, a national phenomenon, a freak of nature, a dynamo on the loose." And Lowell herself once told an admirer, "I enjoy reading poetry to an audience as I should enjoy acting a play to an audience, because it is one side of my genius."[12]

Even the preparations for Lowell's readings were theatrical. Though she was always uncharacteristically punctual for these (arriving with an entourage consisting of Russell, one or two maids, and as many extra hands as needed to carry her props), audiences inevitably waited while first, the traditional slanting lectern was replaced by a large table (which usually had to be carried in over the heads of the audience) so that there was no danger of her papers falling to the floor, out of her reach. Her high-powered reading lamp then had to be plugged in. At one reading, with a horrified Robert Frost standing by, the lamp short-circuited the building's electricity, leaving the two poets to entertain the audience by trading wisecracks in the dark until the lights came back on.[13] During the course of a reading Lowell went through a series of increasingly strong, color-coded pince-nez, which she carried with her in a basket, explaining to the audience, "These are my eyes!" Throughout these preliminaries, she often joked with them, but once she began reading her poems, the audience often didn't know how to respond. She ended their confused silence by admonishing them, with what soon became a trademark phrase, "Well?—Clap or hiss, I don't care which; but for Christ's sake do something!"[14]

The reading lamp, the eyeglasses, the infamous cigars she smoked before and after the readings (and which fans clamored to see), as much as the witty repartee and the intensity of her dramatizations, endowed Lowell's public performances with the thrill of spectacle. Clearly, she was aware of the extent to which these trademarks shaped the general public's perception of her. For example, after reading an early version of an article about herself by Elizabeth Shepley Sergeant she asked that a reference to her smoking a "big black cigar" be removed. Later, she changed her mind, telling Sergeant, "on consideration I think that, in spite of the feeling which still exists on the subject of my cigar, that is one of my characteristics quite as much as my eye-glasses, and as long as everybody knows it, and I am not in the least ashamed of it, I have decided to let you put it back."[15] In addition to appreciating the value of the cigar in bolstering her reputation as a no-nonsense, hard-driving businessperson, she must have recognized the leeway that eccentricity could grant her, a woman whose social class expected her to pursue her artistic interests in private, entering the public sphere only as a supporter of other artists.

It was not only the theatrics of Lowell's readings that shocked some listeners and enthralled others; it was also the *kind* of poetry she read. For although she may have appeared to be following in the footsteps of popular turn-of-the-century literary entertainers like James Whitcomb Riley, Mark Twain, and Oscar Wilde, she was, she continually reminded her listeners, different, representative of an entirely new, *modern* poetry. Lowell took upon herself the task of teaching audiences to appreciate it. If other modernists defined themselves against the vulgar tastes of the masses (as exemplified by Pound's masthead for *The Little Review:* "Making No Compromise with the Public Taste"), Lowell worked to shape and transform them. As she explained to Richard Aldington, chastising him for writing poetry she believed would alienate the average reader, "Great poetry is and must be universal, above the customs and cliques of the initiated."[16]

Not all the audience came to cheer; some came to hiss. Lowell's public lectures and readings inevitably ended in intense debating, with conservative critics accusing her of attempting to destroy poetry. In a letter to Fletcher she describes the atmosphere of her lectures as "a gladiator fight and wild beast show"; C. David Heymann claims audience members were so incensed at the end of one of her readings that they charged the podium.[17] It was not uncommon for the other speakers on the program to abandon their prepared speeches in order to denounce Lowell and the New Poetry, as when one participant accused her of being a "literary hand-grenade thrower." She was more than up to the challenge. Coming from a family of orators and debaters, she relished the conflict: "And then I slammed back good and plenty," she later told Carl Sandburg.[18]

Committing the unpardonable offense of being not only a woman but also a robust woman of wealth and privilege, Lowell was the antithesis of every cherished stereotype of the poet. She once told a newspaper editor, "I started in the world with one of the greatest handicaps that any one could possibly have. I belonged to that class which is not supposed to be able to produce good creative work."[19] While the egregiousness of this comment's insistence on the "difficulty" of being from an upper-class background and wealthy may cause us to wince, she was correct inasmuch as her wealth did seem to shape perceptions of her work and occasionally influenced her self-image.

Still, Lowell was not oblivious to the freedoms that wealth allowed her. By the time she published her first volume of poetry in 1912 her parents had died, her siblings had left to start their own families, and she had bought out their shares in the family home, Sevenels. As the head of her own household, she had the economic wherewithal to eschew social strictures and pursue a career as a professional poet. In a 1919 letter to Winifred Ellerman—a wealthy young British poet, critic, and heir to a railroad fortune, whom she had, until recently, known only by her pen name, Bryher—Lowell counsels the young heiress that it is "just as snobbish to pretend downwards as it is to pretend upwards," and urges her to be herself. "I am Amy Lowell, for better or worse and for all that it implies, and I will not fool myself or the public by play-acting over what to me is the most serious thing in the world—my art." After all, she concludes, "no serious artist wants to go through life as a heroine of romance."[20]

And Amy Lowell was nothing if not serious about her work. As Harriet Monroe puts it, "the force which Miss Lowell's New England ancestors put into founding and running cotton-mills, or belike into saving souls, she [put] into conquering an art and making it express and serve her."[21] Poetry was *the* consuming passion of Lowell's life, and when she wasn't writing it, she was promoting it—both her own and that of her contemporaries whose projects complemented hers, such as H.D., John Gould Fletcher, Robert Frost, D. H. Lawrence, Vachel Lindsay, Edgar Lee Masters, and Carl Sandburg. Her friend, the actress Eleanor Robson Belmont, describes her as "perform[ing] the service of a barker at a circus, as from the lecture platform, in the press, and almost the street corner, she cried aloud, 'Poetry, Poetry, this way to Poetry.'"[22]

Her poetry crackles with an exuberance and zeal that she deliberately refuses to rein in. Responding to William Rose Benét's suggestion that "the time has perhaps come for less sheer abundance, more concentration, a turn or two of the grindstone," Lowell grants his point: "I think you are quite right about the exuberance, and I have been trying to curb it lately." "But," she continues, "I am like an unruly vine, no matter how carefully I tie myself up, I keep splitting and straying all over the lot, with every kind of extraneous-coloured flower at the end of my strayed branches."[23] In a letter to a young poet seeking her advice she defends this poetic dynamism, advising him, "of course we need more beauty in the world; of course that is what we are all fighting for; and, of course, that is what we must make the world safe for. But do not let us lisp this creed in a kind of dying languor; let us shout it lustily—and dare to be happy—and dare to be robust—and dare to be a thousand things which mean poetry just the same."[24]

Oddly, here, in Lowell's joyful, vibrant aesthetic, lies the most common rationalization given for her contemporary neglect. One of her most ardent supporters during her lifetime, Louis Untermeyer, spends an entire chapter of his autobiography describing Lowell's vivacity and charisma, only to close by noting the utter silence and emptiness of the poetry room at Harvard where her manuscripts and papers are collected. Having expected to find Lowell's ghost lurking among her books, he sees and hears nothing. In the same way, the poetry that he once described as "flash[ing], leap[ing], spin[ning] burn[ing] with an almost savage intensity" seems "suddenly lifeless" after her death, "the color . . . superficially applied, the warmth simulated."[25] In other words, Lowell's critical neglect since her death, according to Untermeyer, is in direct proportion to her boisterousness in life: "When she died her poems died with her because they needed her flamboyant personality; they needed all her feminine-masculine vigor."[26] This evaluation has been reiterated over the last three quarters of a century, as in the introduction to one popular anthology of twentieth-century American poetry, in which her influence is neatly dismissed as "less poetic than historical."[27]

Responding to a favorable review of her work by Bryher, Lowell thanked her friend excitedly because she perceived that the British woman *got* her: "You understand both my robustness and my delicacy, and as a rule critics like one or the other but seldom understand the fusion of both."[28] Now, in a time of greater opportunities for women, of increased tolerance for homosexuality, of a loosening of traditional gender roles, her paradoxes no longer trouble. We are ready to appreciate both her "robustness" and her "delicacy," ready to celebrate her "feminine-masculine vigour." At once an effusive lover, a generous mentor, an authoritative critic, and an indefatigable leader, Amy Lowell has much to offer readers in the twenty-first century.

Even a quick glance at her poetry shows Untermeyer's critique to be erroneous—accessible, passionate, moving, her poems retain their immediacy and freshness even without her rich contralto voice reading them. We cannot pinpoint the exact moment when people stopped reading Lowell, or entirely account for the factors that led to the decline of her reputation; we can, however, surmise at least one important reason for conveniently forgetting her: as an independent, outspoken, confident woman who took herself and her career seriously, she posed a serious threat to mid-century ideals of appropriate womanhood. Up until three decades ago few women held a secure place in the literary canon—now canonical female writers like Elizabeth Barrett Browning, Kate Chopin, H.D., and Virginia Woolf are read today only because of vigorous recovery efforts by feminist critics on their behalf. That the difficult and enigmatic Lowell—an imperious, politically conservative, physically imposing lesbian—has not yet made her way back into the spotlight should not surprise us. Thirty years ago we might not have known what to do with Amy Lowell. But today we are ready for her.

## NOTES

1. T. S. Eliot, quoted in David Perkins, *A History of Modern Poetry* (Cambridge: Harvard University Press, 1976), 327.

2. Caption underneath Lowell's picture in an unsigned memorial tribute, "Amy Lowell," in the *Literary Digest,* May 30, 1925, eighteen days after her death.

3. Louis Untermeyer, *American Poetry since 1900* (New York: Henry Holt, 1923), 137.

4. This nickname has often, erroneously, been attributed to Ezra Pound. See Jean Gould, *Amy: The World of Amy Lowell and the Imagist Movement* (New York: Dodd, Mead, 1975), 237; and Ezra Pound, *The Letters of Ezra Pound to Margaret Anderson: The Little Review Correspondence,* ed. Thomas L. Scott and Melvin J. Friedman (New York: New Directions, 1988), 116, where he disavows having coined the name.

5. Elizabeth Shepley Sergeant, "Amy Lowell: Memory Sketch for a Biographer," in *Fire under the Andes: A Group of Literary Portraits* (Port Washington, NY: Kennikat Press, 1966), 16.

6. S. Foster Damon, *Amy Lowell: A Chronicle, with Extracts from Her Correspondence* (Boston: Houghton Mifflin, 1935), 14.

7. Louis Untermeyer, *From Another World: The Autobiography of Louis Untermeyer* (New York: Harcourt Brace, 1939), 107.

8. Amy Lowell, *Tendencies in Modern American Poetry* (New York: Macmillan, 1917), 246.

9. Ibid., 244.

10. Harriet Monroe, *A Poet's Life: Seventy Years in a Changing World* (New York: Macmillan, 1938), 251.

11. Horace Gregory, *Amy Lowell: Portrait of the Poet in Her Time* (New York: Farrar, Straus, and Cudahy, 1957), 122.

12. John Brooks Wheelwright, "Dinner Call," *Collected Poems of John Wheelwright* (New York: New Directions, 1971), 218–20; Van Wyck Brooks, *New England: Indian Summer, 1865–1915* (New York: E.P. Dutton, 1940), 33–34; Untermeyer, *From Another World,* 113; and Gould, *Amy,* 258.

13. Damon, *Amy Lowell,* 392, 602.

14. Gould, *Amy,* 212.

15. Amy Lowell, letter to Elizabeth Shepley Sergeant, April 28, 1922, bMS Lowell 19.1 (1158).

16. Amy Lowell, letter to Richard Aldington, April 11, 1918, bMS Lowell 19.1 (16).

17. Gould, *Amy,* 188; and C. David Heymann, *American Aristocracy: The Lives of James Russell, Amy, and Robert Lowell* (New York: Dodd, Mead, 1980), 212.

18. Amy Lowell, letter to Carl Sandburg, November 25, 1919, bMS 19.1 (1116).

19. Damon, *Amy Lowell,*486.

20. Amy Lowell, letter to Bryher (Winifred Ellerman), January 17, 1917, bMS Lowell 19.1 (180).

21. Harriet Monroe, *Poets and Their Art* (New York: Macmillan, 1926), 79.

22. Eleanor Robson Belmont, *The Fabric of Memory* (New York: Farrar, Straus, and Cudahy, 1957), 187.

23. William Rose Benét, letter to Amy Lowell, June 1915, bMS Lowell 19 (87); Amy Lowell, letter to William Rose Benét, June 1915, bMS Lowell 19.1 (91).

24. Amy Lowell, letter to Donald Evans, June 7, 1918, bMS Lowell 19.1 (452).

25. Untermeyer, *American Poetry,* 152; and *From Another World,* 123.

26. Susan Edmiston and Linda D. Cirino, *Literary New York: A History and Guide* (New York: Houghton Mifflin, 1976), 252.

27. Hayden Carruth, *The Voice That Is Great within Us* (New York: Bantam Books, 1989), xxi.

28. Amy Lowell, letter to Bryher (Winifred Ellerman), November 4, 1918, bMS Lowell 19.1 (180).

# AMY LOWELL,
# NEW AMERICAN POET

*Adrienne Munich*

> I might say with perfect truth that the most national things we
> have are skyscrapers, ice water, and the New Poetry.
>
> —*Amy Lowell, "Is There a National Spirit in*
> *'The New Poetry' of America?"*

AMY LOWELL, sensuous poet of luxuriant textures, was mad for the sights, sounds, and feel of the material universe. For her, both the animate and the inanimate worlds were charged with erotic glory. Her poetry claims for love the power to shape histories, both intimate and public. Her interest in love and sex not only appears in her lyrics but in her history poems, where sexual relationships interweave with world events. History, as she conjures it, is written from the vantage of battles and from the perspective of boudoirs—of Helen of Troy in "The On-looker," of Josephine Bonaparte in "Malmaison," of Emma, Lady Hamilton in "Sea-Blue and Blood-Red," and of Nigi-oi, "courtesan of unrivalled beauty" in "Guns As Keys: And the Great Gate Swings." Her most famous poem, "Patterns," trembles with the unconsummated passion of the speaker, who fantasizes a steamy encounter—a "bodice ripper"—with her lover, who has just died in battle. This is not what people might expect from the stereotype that the label "Boston Brahmin" evokes.

She wrote intimate lyrics about her passionate devotion to the love of her life, Ada Dwyer Russell; she wrote narrative poems about great love affairs and the bustling variety of the city; she wrote elegant translations and imitations of Chinese and Japanese poetry. Lowell saw herself as a modernist, reinventing the word; she was also a modern poet who identified herself with an emerging American democracy of letters. As such, her poetry is comprehensible, welcoming, and clear, particularly in the context of the difficulty of decoding many modernist poets of her generation, such as H.D. (Hilda Doolittle), T. S. Eliot, Ezra Pound, and William Carlos Williams. While it is tempting to link her with her contemporary Gertrude Stein, another great American modernist with a large body, strong opinions, and a faithful beloved, their differences are more instructive. Unlike Stein's experiments with the logic and syntax of American English, Lowell's writing invites all kinds of readers with language that delights not in obscurity but in original combinations and new tempos. The considerably younger New England poet, Edna St. Vincent Millay, published her popular verse at the same time as Lowell's poems, but Millay's poems, unlike her notorious life, do not experiment with formal conventions of language or pattern. Lowell, an equally popular poet, takes risks yet invites readers to share her writing on the edge.

In their volatility and unpredictability the poems can disconcert readers unprepared for an adventure. In *A Critical Fable,* an anonymously published satire of the contemporary poetry scene, Lowell admitted that her poetry might jolt those cherishing the consistency of a measured, well-bred poetic voice: [1]

> Broncho-busting with rainbows is scarcely a game
> For middle-aged persons inclined to the tame. [2]

She warns the unwary that they need to stay alert in order to ride her rhythms. Some minds will be jarred, even tossed off, but some may delight in the adventure.

Three fantastic male figures as embodiments of Lowell's personae suggest the aggressive force required to produce strong effects:

> Armed to the teeth like an old Samurai,
> Juggling with jewels like the ancient genii,

Hung all over with mouse-traps of metres, and cages
Of bright-plumaged rhythms, with pages and pages
Of colours slit up into streaming confetti
Which give the appearance of something sunsetty,
And gorgeous, and flowing—a curious sight
She makes in her progress, a modern White Knight [3]

The most comic of her muses, the White Knight from Lewis Carroll's *Through the Looking Glass* boasted, "I'm a great hand at inventing things," and refers to her poetry's enthusiastic experiments.[4] In fact, the very excesses in this self-portrayal prepare us to expect the unexpected but not the incomprehensible.

Her brand of imagism swept away self-consciously poetic diction in favor of a clean, unadorned, musical line. She wanted to produce a new awareness and to render human senses with a life of their own—and for their own sake. Poetry could find analogies with the direct pleasures of music and painting, as in the dance rhythms of "Gavotte in D Major," or the attempt to put into words the effect of listening to Igor Stravinsky's "Grotesques" for string quartet.

As herald and chronicler of the New Poetry, Lowell saw herself and her kind of imagist poetry as part of a national miracle: "Some fifty years ago, more or less, a handful of unrelated men and women took to being born up and down these United States." Unlike the international turn of other modern writers, she trumpeted a national literature of independence, of a newly forged, motley race that registered its consciousness in different tonalities, but all in a native idiom. Springing out of American soil, these poets responded to a need for a distinctive accent, for characteristic beats that would free America from a colonized mentality and would unite the arts with commerce. Engineers of skyscrapers, inventors of ice water, and new poets emerged from the same national spirit, related to each other by a creative rhythm, that "psychological current which man ignores and invariably obeys."[5]

In the nighttime quiet of her baronial private library, armed with a pistol to ward off intruders and stocked with sandwiches to stave off hunger, Lowell penned new rhythms to express a psychological truth that renounced Victorian reticence. Out of a discovery of her place in a world larger than that of Boston gentility, she staged her liberation from what she saw as its constraining ways. She registered her desire to transform her heritage by imagining a sorority of poets in "The Sisters." In that important poem, the musing poet invites the reader to her nighttime poetry sessions as she encounters her poetic heritage and finds it lacking. Replacing the three male personae of *A Critical Fable,* she looks to three great women poets from whom she might learn her craft: Elizabeth Barrett Browning, Emily Dickinson, and Sappho. She seeks a way to write poetry out of a woman's bodily experiences of its own desires, in its own rhythms. But she does not find what she wants in her greater progenitors. "I cannot write like you," she concludes. At the end of the night the woman poet emerges with renewed consciousness of a need for self-invention. Mousetraps of meters and bright-plumaged rhythms declare that independence in an attempt to join a rich family heritage to the dynamic American poetry scene.

Imagism became that link, presenting the material surface of the perceived world closely and intimately observed. This "objective" bias does not lead to dry, cerebral poetry; tightly wrought description not only produces a glittering surface—as she says gorgeous, and flowing—but also deep emotion. Often, as in "Opal," the description of the gem's flashing lights emerges from the speaker's passion. The imagist emblem acts as a threshold to vividly rendered sensuous imagery: the taste of a beloved; the sight of a firelit or moonlit or sunlit body; the symbolic center holding through the cadences. In "The Captured Goddess," Lowell strews color images in an ecstatic catalog. The dazzling effect leads to more than just pyrotechnics; profusion of closely observed colors evokes a glorious divinity.

While her historical narratives may surprise with their vehement politics mingled with nostalgic passion, her erotic lyrics may startle with sensuous imagery and overflowing emotions. Lyrical joy is often accompanied by a sense of fervent wonder at a beloved who illuminates landscapes as no moon could. The daring erotic lyrics often describe things as objectifications of deeply felt emotion, as in the sense of heated suspension in "The Blue Scarf":

A jar of green jade throws its shadow half over the floor. A
   big-bellied
Frog hops through the sunlight and plops in the gold-bubbled
   water of a basin . . .

Globes of water catch the heated sunlight, disturbed by that plump
frog in a deeply sexualized garden scene, saturated with desire. Lo-
well's flowers (as magnified as those in Georgia O'Keefe's paintings
of the same period) are equally charged—for instance, in "Au-
bade" and "The Weathervane Points South."

The poems in this volume are organized according to some of
Lowell's characteristic forms, from the more traditional to the most
experimental. In each section they appear in chronological order,
reproducing the largely unavailable texts that appeared for the
most part in a wide range of periodicals. We begin with sonnets—
Lowell's first published poems, and also some of her last. When
she wrote as an apologist for modern poetry, she wrote of sonnets
as if they were too old-fashioned for authentic moderns. In a ri-
poste to a critic who yearned for traditional poetic forms rather
than free verse and polyphonic prose, Lowell speaks of the sonnet
form as if only the nostalgic reader would desire it: "Mr. Warner
and his ilk should take heart in the thought that possibly in a hun-
dred years or so, poets will be rediscovering the sonnet and glory-
ing in its practice."[6] But before and after her jab at the benighted
Warners of her world, she herself wrote fine sonnets.

Her first published poem, "A Fixed Idea," shows the poet work-
ing with characteristic themes of the love sonnet tradition: tor-
mented love compared with its comforts, the lover's conflicting
desires for self-abasement and mastery. Its fierce ending—"In
mercy lift your drooping wings and go"—foreshadows other blunt
and forceful lines in later poems. "The Starling," another early and
poignant sonnet, expresses in the strict form a romantic yet the-
matically characteristic discomfort of the poet with the constric-
tions of life, the imprisoned soul longing to shed constraints to live
out "alien passions," "strange imaginings." The sonnet form allows
the poet to announce her own alien passions, the form itself sug-
gesting the constraints of her immensely privileged social world.

Although sonnets could not satisfy Lowell's experimental, risk-taking temperament, the formal requirements did enable her to express the thematic conflict between restraint and independence, a theme in many poems using other forms. She teases the reader in "In Answer to a Request" for a sonnet by choosing among the most conventional rhymes in the lyricist's repertory—noon, June, moon—but then with a surprise and subversive fifteenth line, she ends the expanded sonnet with a blazing impression of the lover's utter devotion: "I cannot turn, the light would make me blind." At the same time, the extra line signals the lover's independence or at least deviance from a settled form—and also from a beloved's demands. Late in her career, Lowell chose the sonnet form to honor the artist who inspired her vocation, compelling her to write poetry—the great dramatic actress Eleonora Duse. Published in *The New Republic* in 1924, right after the actress's death and a year before Lowell's own, the moving sonnet sequence "Eleonora Duse" pays homage to the actress.

To distance herself from venerable Western poetic forms placed her in a modern avant garde; to embrace ancient Eastern forms appeared to create something new for modernist poetry. China and Japan acted, to adapt Robert Browning's notorious phrase about Italy, as "stuff for the West"—poetic commodities to cart home and use. With characteristic energy Lowell explored the poetic conventions of the Orient without traveling there or even knowing its languages. Her older brother Percival (Percy) had lived in Japan and had written four books on the East, dating from the year after Amy's birth to 1895, when she was twenty-one years old. Her early connections to Japan led to her collaboration with a school friend, Florence Wheelock Ayscough, who was born and then later lived in China, becoming a prominent specialist in Chinese literary language. Ayscough rendered literal translations, Lowell transformed them into poems, and after years of work, they collected and published the results in *Fir-Flower Tablets* (1921). These powerfully beautiful translations place Lowell at the forefront of imagist poets who looked to Asia for inspiration, and, together with her adapted Asian forms, constitute a major contribution to modernism.

In addition to reflecting the general influence of Asian aesthetics on modernism, Lowell came to her interest in China through the China trade that was a part of her heritage. New Englanders made fortunes trading goods from the East, and poets also cashed in on the deal. Her celebration of the New England landscape in "Meeting-House Hill" reveals that deep familiarity. Clipper ships limned in typical seascapes were often bound for or returning from the Orient:

I might be sighting a tea-clipper,
Tacking into the blue bay,
Just back from Canton
With her hold full of green and blue porcelain [. . . .]

With the intimacy of her valuable personal contacts, Lowell found herself "charmed" with Asian poetry, the word itself indicating an exotic spell. We have included here some of her translations and some Asian-influenced forms, along with a few poems that seem directly orientalist in spirit, with their mention of flowers associated with Asia—camellias and peonies—and the austere notation of smells, sounds, and sights. Such poems as "Nostalgia," "Vespers," and "Afterglow" illustrate close affinities between imagism and Western notions of Chinese poetry. Lowell's involvement with Asian forms was not limited to lyrics. In a poem in polyphonic prose, "Guns As Keys: And the Great Gate Swings," about Commodore Matthew Perry's opening up American trade with Japan, the poetic rhythms evoke the historic confrontation by alternating a muscular, often crude, tempo for the American West with a lyrical, elegant cadence for the Japanese East.

Adapting Asian forms and reading French *vers libre* and the poetry of her great progenitors, Emily Dickinson and Walt Whitman, gave Lowell precedent for her most characteristic form, free verse, or her preferred term, *cadenced verse,* which we have adopted here. In her view, this kind of rhythmic verse freed poetry to express the American race, to write America. Cadenced verse resembles breathing. Readers inhale and exhale essential life rhythms in their own idiom. This form, used by imagism but not limited to it, determined the shape of most of her poetry.

According to Lowell's strictures, "Cadence is rhythm. Modern *vers libre,* far from being non-rhythmical as some people have supposed, is entirely based upon rhythm. Its rhythms differ from those of metre by being less obvious and more subtle, but rhythm is, nevertheless, the very ground and root of its structure."[7] When read aloud, these lines from "White and Green" echo and gather in rhythmic intensity from repeated vowels, consonants, and parts of speech, arranged in varied patterns:

> You are an almond flower unsheathed
> Leaping and flickering between the budded branches.

The verse seems open-ended, but once felt, Lowell's poems open themselves to rich, sensuous experience, held together by an unwavering grasp of a central symbol.

"Thompson's Lunch Room—Grand Central Station," illustrates the power of what Lowell called a "contrapuntal and various tone." She would have considered it a narrative poem, with the lunchroom objects functioning as dramatic personae. In harnessing the power of the other arts, it is a quintessential modern poem; it captures a mundane city scene as a still life, but with movement, where commonplace food is consumed as a visual symphony, mostly in white. It is a story of ordinary objects in a common lunchroom. Inspired by the American painter James McNeill Whistler, from whom she bought a painting, the poem recalls his focus on color and his analogies to music, reflected in such titles as *Nocturne in Black and Gold—Old Battersea Bridge,* his cityscape of warehouses on the Thames. The poem also contrasts with the vision of the moody rendering of a diner at night, as depicted in the New England painter Edward Hopper's *Nighthawks.* "Thompson's Lunchroom," however, characteristically celebrates the sensuous pleasure of hard objects and food displays, as well as intimates a melancholy awareness of time passing.

The last section of the book offers a sample of "polyphonic prose," an invention Lowell was led to by the efforts of the French poet Paul Fort to break up the French alexandrine. Into polyphonic prose Lowell incorporates some imagist tenets, such as "to create new rhythms" and "absolute freedom in choice of subjects." Polyphonic prose combines lyric passages with narrative, rhyme with cadenced verse, and personal perspectives with grand historical events: of all forms, she considered it the most liberating, as it offered a full linguistic and formal spectrum, resembling mixed media in art or a symphony orchestra in music: "'Polyphonic prose' is the freest, the most elastic, of all forms, for it follows at will any, and all, of the rules which guide other forms," she explained in the preface to *Can Grande's Castle,* the volume that successfully introduced a large number of polyphonic poems to a receptive audience. "Metrical verse has one set of laws, cadenced verse another; 'polyphonic prose' can go from one to the other in the same poem with no sense of incongruity."[8]

Because polyphonic prose might seem visually indistinguishable from prose, Lowell asserts that poetry "is not a matter of typography; it is a matter of approach and of return . . . some device by which a poem is brought continually back to its starting-place—something which keeps the basic emotional symbol constantly reappearing throughout the poem. . . . There are as many ways of achieving 'return' as there are prosodies, but in every one it is the determining factor of the technique of poetry."[9] So, for instance, in the "Bath" section of the poem "Spring Day," for which she was ridiculed (readers felt forced to contemplate a naked mature fat woman cavorting in a sunlit bathtub) the poet closely observes the play of light in water:

> The sunshine pours in at the bath-room window and bores
> through the water in the bath-tub in lathes and planes of
> greenish-white. It cleaves the water into flaws like a jewel, and
> cracks it to bright light.

Sensuality and pleasure involve violence; sounds and images return, clash, and coalesce. Water's activity, like a warrior, invades the body's tranquility, while the artist's body, working with nature and as a shaper of form, pushes back: "a stir of my finger sets them whirring, reeling."

Return structures "Malmaison," a polyphonic poem about Napoleon Bonaparte's abandonment of his wife Josephine. Sun striking the slate roof of their home, Malmaison, returns as an image of emotional violence, as do the clouds blowing across the sky "like ships of the line, stately with canvas," transforming in meaning each time the same words return, like a chorus. Josephine's favorite roses, rich with traditional erotic symbolism, appear in bloom, first as descriptions, returning as a metaphor for the female sexual body, then finally as a crumpled but tender sign of age and loss.

The collective effect of "Sea-Blue and Blood-Red," focusing on the love triangle of Admiral Horatio Nelson; William, Lord Hamilton; and Emma, Lady Hamilton illustrates how Lowell used polyphonic prose to capture private nuances of history: its setting, its characters, particularly physical sensations. Under the glare of the Mediterranean sun in Naples and Egypt, the sea, sky, and volcano are as much dramatis personae as the human characters. Lowell's description of the sea prefigures human drives as they mingle with large geopolitical and natural forces. Having established symbolic connections between Lady Hamilton and the simmering Vesuvius, the famous volcano also becomes associated with graphically described scenes of carnage associated with war. Sparks from the volcano become a potent symbol of the personal and political eruptions that are the subject of the poem, returning as a landscape where red invades the blue of the sky, the glare of the water. In one scene, the three human actors cast adrift on the Bay of Naples represent all that is fragile as the tiny figures merge and glow with the surround.

The wide sweep of history could be considered a kind of return structuring Lowell's vision, from the cosmos of the universe to the microcosm of the home, the street, the flower. Her kinds of poetry offer pleasure to a wide range of readers' tastes. Because of its variety, Amy Lowell's work cannot be swallowed whole, true as well of those other profuse American poets, Whitman and Dickinson, whose voices also spoke against the grain. Lowell, by the way, considered Dickinson an imagist *avant la lettre* and Whitman an unconscious writer of cadenced verse. She helped to build the road leading to Allen Ginsberg, May Sarton, and Sylvia Plath, and beyond. Yet until now, readers have not been able to find a representative selection from this vigorous, courageous poet who gave voice to an erotic, thoroughly American sensibility. Her own enthusiastic promotions prepared the times for herself—a cigar-smoking Boston Brahmin, lesbian lover, impresario, entrepreneur, and prolific poet who could herald, in italics, the rush of an American poetic flowering: "*All of a sudden there leapt into the world a new poetry.*" [10] The time has come to reencounter Amy Lowell's supremely energetic poetic voice.

## NOTES

1. The title is a sly reference to her distant relative, James Russell Lowell, whose legacy she resisted, even resented. Nevertheless, her title echoes his *A Fable for Critics.*

2. A Poker of Fun [Amy Lowell], *A Critical Fable* (Boston: Houghton Mifflin, 1922), 47.

3. Ibid., 49.

4. Lewis Carroll, chapter 8 of *Through the Looking Glass,* facsimile ed. (New York: Alfred A. Knopf, 1984), 168.

5. Amy Lowell, "Two Generations in American Poetry," in *Poetry and Poets* (Boston: Houghton Mifflin, 1930), 112; 113.

6. Amy Lowell, "In Defence of *Vers Libre,*" *The Dial* (September 7, 1916): 133.

7. Amy Lowell, "Walt Whitman and the New Poetry," in *Poetry and Poets* (Boston: Houghton Mifflin, 1930), 70.

8. Amy Lowell, preface to *Can Grande's Castle* (Boston: Houghton Mifflin, 1918), x.

9. Lowell, "Walt Whitman," 71.

10. Amy Lowell, "Is There a National Spirit in 'The New Poetry' of America?" *The Craftsman* 30 (July 1916): 339–49.

# CHRONOLOGY

1874    • February 9, born in Brookline, Massachusetts, youngest child of Augustus Lowell and Katherine Bigelow Lawrence Lowell.

1887    • *Dream Drops, or Stories from Fairyland* coauthored with her mother and her sister, Elizabeth Lowell; privately printed, and sold at a Faneuil Hall Fair, Boston, Massachusetts, with profits donated to the Perkins Institution and Massachusetts School for the Blind.

1890–91    • Final year of her formal education; sometime during this year she finds Leigh Hunt's *Imagination and Fancy* on her father's bookshelf, which introduces her to the poetry of John Keats.

1895    • Her mother dies.

1897–98    • Spends winter traveling down the Nile in a small boat with two friends and a retinue of servants. The intense Egyptian heat and a strict diet of asparagus and tomatoes were intended as a weight-loss regimen.

1899    • Lives in Southern California at the estate of her friend, Frances Dabney, recovering from "nervous prostration" and the gastric effects of the Egyptian journey (which would cause her to suffer for the next seven years).

1900    • Her father dies.
        • Purchases family estate, Sevenels, from siblings and settles permanently in Brookline.

| | |
|---|---|
| *1902* | • Performance by Italian actress Eleonora Duse inspires her to decide on poetry as her vocation; begins rigorous self-education in poetry and poetics. |
| *1909* | • March 25, a fire destroys Sevenels' stables and all its horses; anonymous letters over the next several days suggest arson, and that the Lowells had been targeted because of their suppression of union activity in their mills and factories; the poet subsequently purchases a revolver, which she keeps on her desk as she writes at night. |
| | • Her brother, Abbot Lawrence Lowell, becomes president of Harvard University. |
| *1910* | • Publishes first poem, the sonnet "A Fixed Idea," in *The Atlantic Monthly*. |
| *1912* | • *A Dome of Many-Coloured Glass.* |
| | • March 12, meets actress Ada Dwyer Russell, who passes through Boston touring with the play *The Deep Purple*. |
| *1913* | • Travels to London, meets Richard Aldington, H.D., John Gould Fletcher, Henry James, D. H. Lawrence, and Ezra Pound. |
| | • The poet's love of cigars becomes news when she is observed smoking during her return trip across the Atlantic; arrives in Boston to outraged nationwide newspaper reports that the sister of President Lowell of Harvard smokes cigars. |
| *1914* | • *Sword Blades and Poppy Seed.* |
| | • "In a Garden" included in Pound's *Des Imagistes* anthology. |
| | • In June, Ada Dwyer Russell accepts the poet's invitation to live with her at Sevenels. |
| | • Returns to England, where she meets Thomas Hardy. |
| | • Becomes stranded in England during the first months of World War I. |
| | • Convinces Houghton Mifflin to issue a New Poetry series that will publish eighteen volumes over the next three years, including her imagist anthologies. |

- December 17, gives first public reading, at Steinert Hall in Boston.

1915
- *Six French Poets.*
- *Some Imagist Poets* (editor).
- In February, performance of two French operettas, *Pierrot Qui Pleure et Pierrot Qui Rit* and *La Latière de Trianon*, translated and produced by the poet for performance by the Boston Women's Municipal League, accompanied by the Boston Opera Orchestra.
- March 31, first public battle over New Poetry when she promotes *Some Imagist Poets* at the annual meeting of the Poetry Society of America. The poet's comments so enrage audience members that they charge the podium when she finishes speaking.

1916
- *Men, Women and Ghosts.*
- *Some Imagist Poets II* (editor).
- Travels to New York and Chicago for first lecture tour.
- In the summer, tears stomach muscles in a carriage accident.
- In October, overwork leads to neuralgia, gastritis, and jaundice; spends a month bedridden and sedated with morphine, too sick to be told of the sudden death of her older brother, Percival Lowell, on November 13.

1917
- *Tendencies in Modern American Poetry.*
- *Some Imagist Poets III* (editor).
- Two lecture tours, much more extensive than the previous year, include stops in Brooklyn, New York; Princeton, New Jersey; St. Louis, Missouri; Chicago, Illinois; Cincinnati, Ohio; and Buffalo, New York.

1918
- *Can Grande's Castle.*
- Reinjures stomach muscles, resulting in an umbilical hernia.
- In September, the first of four operations over the next two years attempts to repair the hernia.

1919
- *Pictures of the Floating World.*

- The poet's last public fight over the New Poetry, at the Contemporary Club of Philadelphia's celebration of the Walt Whitman centenary.

1920
- Bestowed with an honorary doctorate in literature at Baylor University, Waco, Texas.

1921
- *Legends.*
- *Fir-Flower Tablets* (with Florence Ayscough).

1922
- *A Critical Fable,* published under the pseudonym A Poker of Fun.

1925
- *John Keats.*
- May 12, the poet recognizes her imminent death from a stroke when she sees the right side of her face drop while looking in a mirror at home in Brookline; she dies a half hour later.
- May 15, her ashes are placed in the Lowell family plot, Mount Auburn Cemetery, Boston.

1925
- *What's O' Clock.*

1926
- May 3, posthumously awarded Pulitzer Prize for *What's O' Clock.*
- *East Wind.*

1927
- *Ballads for Sale.*

1930
- *Poetry and Poets,* a collection of previously unpublished essays and lectures.

# Selected Poems of Amy Lowell

# TRADITIONAL
# FORMS AND
# VARIATIONS

We should read poetry because only in that way can we
know man in all his moods—in the most beautiful thoughts
of his heart, in his farthest reaches of imagination, in the tenderness
of his love, in the nakedness and awe of his soul confronted
with the terror and wonder of the Universe.

—AMY LOWELL, "Why We Should Read Poetry"

# SONNETS, RHYMED STANZAS, AND BLANK VERSE

Great emotion always tends to become rhythmic, and out of that
tendency the forms of art have been evolved. Art becomes artificial
only when the forms take precedence over the emotion.

—Amy Lowell, *Tendencies in Modern American Poetry*

## A FIXED IDEA

What torture lurks within a single thought
When grown too constant; and however kind,
However welcome still, the weary mind
Aches with its presence. Dull remembrance taught
Remembers on unceasingly; unsought
The old delight is with us but to find
That all recurring joy is pain refined,
Become a habit, and we struggle, caught.
You lie upon my heart as on a nest,
Folded in peace, for you can never know
How crushed I am with having you at rest
Heavy upon my life. I love you so
You bind my freedom from its rightful quest.
In mercy lift your drooping wings and go.

*The Atlantic Monthly,* August 1910

## ON CARPACCIO'S PICTURE:
## THE DREAM OF ST. URSULA

Swept, clean, and still, across the polished floor
    From some unshuttered casement, hid from sight,
    The level sunshine slants, its greater light
Quenching the little lamp which pallid, poor,
Flickering, unreplenished, at the door
    Has striven against darkness the long night.
    Dawn fills the room, and penetrating, bright,
The silent sunbeams through the window pour.
    And she lies sleeping, ignorant of Fate,
    Enmeshed in listless dreams, her soul not yet
Ripened to bear the purport of this day.
    The morning breeze scarce stirs the coverlet,
    A shadow falls across the sunlight; wait!
A lark is singing as he flies away.

The Atlantic Monthly, September 1911

## THE STARLING

"'I can't get out,' said the starling."
STERNE'S Sentimental Journey

Forever the impenetrable wall
    Of self contains my poor rebellious soul,
    I never see the towering white clouds roll
Before a sturdy wind, save through the small
Barred window of my jail. I live a thrall
    With all my outer life a clipped, square hole,
    Rectangular; a fraction of a scroll
Unwound and winding like a worsted ball.
    My thoughts are grown uneager and depressed
    Through being always mine; my fancy's wings

Are moulted, and the feathers blown away.
  I weary for desires never guessed,
  For alien passions, strange imaginings,
To be some other person for a day.

*The Atlantic Monthly,* July 1912

## MIRAGE

How is it that, being gone, you fill my days,
  And all the long nights are made glad by thee?
  No loneliness is this, nor misery,
But great content that these should be the ways
Whereby the Fancy, dreaming as she strays,
  Makes bright and present what she would would be.
  And who shall say if the reality
Is not with dreams so pregnant. For delays
  And hindrances may bar the wished-for end;
A thousand misconceptions may prevent
  Our souls from coming near enough to blend;
Let me but think we have the same intent,
  That each one needs to call the other, "friend!"
It may be vain illusion. I'm content.

*A Dome of Many-Coloured Glass,* October 1912

## A PETITION

I pray to be the tool which to your hand
  Long use has shaped and moulded till it be
  Apt for your need, and, unconsideringly,
You take it for its service. I demand
To be forgotten in the woven strand
  Which grows the multi-coloured tapestry
  Of your bright life, and through its tissues lie

A hidden, strong, sustaining, grey-toned band.
   I wish to dwell around your daylight dreams,
The railing to the stairway of the clouds,
   To guard your steps securely up, where streams
A faëry moonshine washing pale the crowds
   Of pointed stars. Remember not whereby
   You mount, protected, to the far-flung sky.

*Sword Blades and Poppy Seed,* September 1914

## IN ANSWER TO A REQUEST

You ask me for a sonnet. Ah, my Dear,
   Can clocks tick back to yesterday at noon?
   Can cracked and fallen leaves recall last June
And leap up on the boughs, now stiff and sere?
For your sake, I would go and seek the year,
   Faded beyond the purple ranks of dune,
   Blown sands of drifted hours, which the moon
Streaks with a ghostly finger, and her sneer
   Pulls at my lengthening shadow. Yes 'tis that!
   My shadow stretches forward, and the ground
Is dark in front because the light's behind.
   It is grotesque, with such a funny hat,
   In watching it and walking I have found
More than enough to occupy my mind.

I cannot turn, the light would make me blind.

*Sword Blades and Poppy Seed,* September 1914

## ELEONORA DUSE

I.
Seeing's believing, so the ancient word
Chills buds to shrivelled powder flecks, turns flax

To smoky heaps of straw whose small flames wax
Only to gasp and die. The thing's absurd!
Have blind men ever seen or deaf men heard?
What one beholds but measures what one lacks.
Where is the prism to draw gold from blacks,
Or flash the iris colours of a bird?
Not in the eye, be sure, nor in the ear,
Nor in an instrument of twisted glass,
Yet there are sights I see and sounds I hear
Which ripple me like water as they pass.
This that I give you for a dear love's sake
Is curling noise of waves marching along a lake.

II.
A letter or a poem—the words are set
To either tune. Be careful how you slice
The flap which is held down by this device
Impressed upon it. In one moment met
A cameo, intaglio, a fret
Of workmanship, and I. Like melted ice
I took the form and froze so, turned precise
And brittle seal, a creed in silhouette.
Seeing's believing? What then would you see?
A chamfered dragon? Three spear-beads of steel?
A motto done in flowered charactry?
The thin outline of Mercury's winged heel?
Look closer, do you see a name, a face,
Or just a cloud dropped down before a holy place?

III.
Lady, to whose enchantment I took shape
So long ago, though carven to your grace,
Bearing, like quickened wood, your sweet sad face
Cut in my flesh, yet may I not escape
My limitations: words that jibe and gape
After your loveliness and make grimace
And travesty where they should interlace

The weave of sun-spun ocean round a cape.
Pictures then must contain you, this and more,
The sigh of wind floating on ripe June hay,
The desolate pulse of snow beyond a door,
The grief of mornings seen as yesterday.
All that you are mingles as one sole cry
To point a world aright which is so much awry.

IV.

If Beauty set her image on a stage
And bid it mirror moments so intense
With passion and swift largess of the sense
To a divine exactness, stamp a page
With mottoes of hot blood, and disengage
No atom of mankind's experience,
But lay the soul's complete incontinence
Bare while it tills grief's gusty acreage.
Doing this, you, spon-image to her needs,
She picked to pierce, reveal, and soothe again,
Shattering by means of you the tinsel creeds
Offered as meat to the pinched hearts of men.
So, sacrificing you, she fed those others
Who bless you in their prayers even before their mothers.

V.

Life seized you with her iron hands and shook
The fire of your boundless burning out
To fall on us, poor little ragged rout
Of common men, till like a flaming book
We, letters of a message, flashed and took
The fiery flare of prophecy, devout
Torches to bear your oil, a dazzling shout,
The liquid golden running of a brook.
Who, being upborne on racing streams of light,
Seeing new heavens sprung from dusty hells,
Considered you, and what might be your plight,
Robbed, plundered—since Life's cruel plan compels

The perfect sacrifice of one great soul
To make a myriad others even a whit more whole.

VI.
Seeing you stand once more before my eyes
In your pale dignity and tenderness,
Wearing your frailty like a misty dress
Draped over the great glamour which denies
To years their domination, all disguise
Time can achieve is but to add a stress,
A finer fineness, as though some caress
Touched you a moment to a strange surprise.
Seeing you after these long lengths of years,
I only know the glory come again,
A majesty bewildered by my tears,
A golden sun spangling slant shafts of rain,
Moonlight delaying by a sick man's bed,
A rush of daffodils where wastes of dried leaves spread.

*This sonnet sequence was written several months ago, in contemplation of Signora Duse's proposed final appearences in New York, which were to have taken place early in May.*

*The New Republic,* April 30, 1924


## TO A LADY OF UNDENIABLE BEAUTY
## AND PRACTISED CHARM

No peacock strutting on a balustrade
Could air his feathers with a cooler grace,
Assume a finer insolence of pace,
Or make his sole advance a cavalcade
Of sudden shifts of colour, slants of shade,
Than you, the cold indifference of your face
Sharpening the cunning lure of velvets, lace,
Greens, blues, and golds, seduction on parade.
You take the accolade of staring eyes

As something due your elegance of pose,
Feeding your vanity on pecks of dust,
The weary iteration which supplies
No zest. I see you as a cankered rose
Its silver petals curled and cracked with rust.

*Saturday Review of Literature,* October 17, 1925

## BEFORE THE ALTAR

Before the Altar, bowed, he stands
With empty hands;
Upon it perfumed offerings burn
Wreathing with smoke the sacrificial urn.
Not one of all these has he given,
No flame of his has leapt to Heaven
Firesouled, vermilion-hearted,
Forked, and darted,
Consuming what a few spare pence
Have cheaply bought, to fling from hence
In idly-asked petition.

His sole condition
Love and poverty.
And while the moon
Swings slow across the sky,
Athwart a waving pine tree,
And soon
Tips all the needles there
With silver sparkles, bitterly
He gazes, while his soul
Grows hard with thinking of the poorness of his dole.

"Shining and distant Goddess, hear my prayer
Where you swim in the high air!
With charity look down on me,

Under this tree,
Tending the gifts I have not brought,
The rare and goodly things
I have not sought.
Instead, take from me all my life!

"Upon the wings
Of shimmering moonbeams
I pack my poet's dreams
For you.
My wearying strife,
My courage, my loss,
Into the night I toss
For you.
Golden Divinity,
Deign to look down on me
Who so unworthily
Offers to you:
All life has known,
Seeds withered unsown,
Hopes turning quick to fears,
Laughter which dies in tears.
The shredded remnant of a man
Is all the span
And compass of my offering to you.

"Empty and silent, I
Kneel before your pure, calm majesty.
On this stone, in this urn
I pour my heart and watch it burn,
Myself the sacrifice; but be
Still unmoved: Divinity."

From the altar, bathed in moonlight,
The smoke rose straight in the quiet night.

*A Dome of Many-Coloured Glass*, October 1912

APOLOGY

Be not angry with me that I bear
  Your colours everywhere,
  All through each crowded street,
    And meet
  The wonder-light in every eye,
    As I go by.

Each plodding wayfarer looks up to gaze,
  Blinded by rainbow haze,
  The stuff of happiness,
    No less,
  Which wraps me in its glad-hued folds
    Of peacock golds.

Before my feet the dusty, rough-paved way
  Flushes beneath its gray.
  My steps fall ringed with light,
    So bright,
  It seems a myriad suns are strown
    About the town.

Around me is the sound of steepled bells,
  And rich perfumed smells
  Hang like a wind-forgotten cloud,
    And shroud
  Me from close contact with the world.
    I dwell impearled.

You blazon me with jewelled insignia.
  A flaming nebula
  Rims in my life. And yet
    You set
  The word upon me, unconfessed
    To go unguessed.

*Poetry,* July 1913

## AFTER WRITING "THE BRONZE HORSES"

I am so tired.
I have run across the ages with spiritless feet,
I have tracked man where he falls splintered in defeat,
I have watched him shoot up like green sprouts at dawning,
I have seen him blossom, and fruit, and offer himself, fawning,
On golden platters to kings.
I have seen him reel with drunk blood,
I have followed him in flood
Sweep over his other selves.
I have written things
Which sucked the breath
Out of my lungs, and hung
My heart up in a frozen death.
I have picked desires
Out of purple fires
And set them on the shelves
Of my mind,
Nonchalantly,
As though my kind
Were unlike these.
But while I did this, my bowels contracted in twists of fear.
I felt myself squeeze
Myself dry,
And wished that I could shrivel before Destiny
Could snatch me back into the vortex of Yesterday.
Wheels and wheels—
And only your hand is firm.
The very paths of my garden squirm
Like snakes between the brittle flowers,
And the sunrise gun cuts off the hours
Of this day and the next.
The long, dusty volumes are the first lines of a text.
Oh, Beloved, must we read?
Must you and I, alone in the midst of trees,
See their green alleys printing with the screed

Which counts these new men, these
Terrible resurrections of old wars.
I wish I had not seen so much:
The roses that you wear are bloody scars,
And you the moon above a battle-field;
So all my thoughts are grown to such.
A body peeled
Down to a skeleton,
A grinning jaw-bone in a bed of mignonette.
What good is it to say "Not yet."
I tell you I am tired
And afraid.

*Pictures of the Floating World*, September 1919


## MERELY STATEMENT

You sent me a sprig of mignonette,
Cool-colored, quiet, and it was wet
With green sea-spray, and the salt and the sweet
Mingled to a fragrance weary and discreet
As a harp played softly in a great room at sunset.

You said: "My sober mignonette
Will brighten your room and you will not forget."

But I have pressed your flower and laid it away
In a letter, tied with a ribbon knot.
I have not forgot.
But there is a passion-flower in my vase
Standing above a close-cleared space
In the midst of a jumble of papers and books.

The passion-flower holds my eyes,
And the light-under-light of its blue and purple dyes
Is a hot surprise.
How then can I keep my looks
From the passion-flower leaning sharply over the books?

When one has seen
The difficult magnificence of a queen
On one's table,
Is one able
To observe any color in a mignonette?
I will not think of sunset, I crave the dawn,
With its rose-red light on the wings of a swan,
And a queen pacing slowly through the Parthenon,
Her dress a stare of purple between pillars of stone.

*The Bookman,* May 1920


## GAVOTTE IN D MINOR

She wore purple, and when other people slept
She stept lightly—lightly—in her ruby powdered slippers
Along the flags of the East portico.
And the moon slowly rifting the heights of cloud
Touched her face so that she bowed
Her head, and held her hand to her eyes
To keep the white shining from her. And she was wise,
For gazing at the moon was like looking on her own dead face
Passing alone in a wide place,
Chill and uncosseted, always above
The hot protuberance of life. Love to her
Was morning and a great stir
Of trumpets and tire-women and sharp sun.
As she had begun, so she would end,
Walking alone to the last bend
Where the portico turned the wall.
And her slipper's sound
Was scarce as loud upon the ground
As her tear's fall.
Her long white fingers crisped and clung
Each to each, and her weary tongue
Rattled always the same cold speech:
    "Gold was not made to lie in grass,

Silver dints at the touch of brass,
  The days pass."

Lightly, softly, wearily,
The lady paces, drearily
Listening to the half-shrill croon
Leaves make on a moony Autumn night
When the windy light
Runs over the ivy eerily.
A branch at the corner cocks an obscene eye
As she passes—passes—by and by—
A hand stretches out from a column's edge,
Faces float in a phosphorent wedge
Through the points of arches, and there is speech
In the carven roof-groins out of reach.
A love-word, a lust-word, shivers and mocks
The placid stroke of the village clocks.
Does the lady hear?
Is any one near?
She jeers at life, must she wed instead
The cold dead?
A marriage-bed of moist green mold,
With an over-head tester of beaten gold.
A splendid price for a splendid scorn,
A tombstone pedigree snarled with thorn
Clouding the letters and the fleur-de-lis,
She will have them in granite for her heart's chill ease.

I set the candle in a draught of air
And watched it swale to the last thin flair.
They laid her in a fair chamber hung with arras,
And they wept her virgin soul.
The arras was woven of the story of Minos and Dictynna.
But I grieved that I could no longer hear the shuffle of her feet
    along the portico,
And the ruffling of her train against the stones.

*The Dial,* June 1920

## SONG FOR A VIOLA D'AMORE

The lady of my choice is bright
As a clematis at the touch of night,
As a white clematis with a purple heart
When twilight cuts earth and sun apart.
Through the dusking garden I hear her voice
As a smooth, sweet, wandering, windy noise,
And I see her stand as a ghost may do
In answer to a rendezvous
Long sought with agony and prayer.
So watching her, I see her there.
I sit beneath a quiet tree
And watch her everlastingly.
The garden may or may not be
Before my eyes, I cannot see.
But darkness drifting up and down
Divides to let her silken gown
Gleam there beside the clematis.
How marvellously white it is!
Five white blossoms and she are there
Like candles in a fluttering air
Escaping from a tower stair.

*Be still you cursed, rattling leaf,*
*This is no time to think of grief.*

The night is soft, and fireflies
Are very casual, gay, and wise,
And they have made a tiny glee
Just where the clematis and she
Are standing. Since the sky is clear,
Do they suppose that, once a year,
The moon and five white stars appear
Walking the earth; that, so attended,
Diana came and condescended

To hold speech with Endymion
Before she came at last alone?

The lady of my choice is bright
As a clematis at the fall of night.
Her voice is honeysuckle sweet,
Her presence spreads an April heat
Before the going of her feet.
She is of perfectness complete,
The lady whom my heart perceives
As a clematis above its leaves,
As a purple-hearted clematis.
And what is lovelier than that is?

*Harper's,* November 1922

## NUIT BLANCHE

I want no horns to rouse me up to-night,
And trumpets make too clamorous a ring
To fit my mood, it is so weary white
I have no wish for doing any thing.

A music coaxed from humming strings would please;
Not plucked, but drawn in creeping cadences
Across a sunset wall where some Marquise
Picks a pale rose amid strange silences.

Ghostly and vaporous her gown sweeps by
The twilight dusking wall, I hear her feet
Delaying on the gravel, and a sigh,
Briefly permitted, touches the air like sleet

And it is dark, I hear her feet no more.
A red moon leers beyond the lily-tank.
A drunken moon ogling a sycamore,
Running long fingers down its shining flank.

A lurching moon, as nimble as a clown,
Cuddling the flowers and trees which burn like glass.
Red, kissing lips, I feel you on my gown—
Kiss me, red lips, and then pass—pass.

Music, you are pitiless to-night.
And I so old, so cold, so languorously white.

*Double Dealer,* February 1923

## ON LOOKING AT A COPY OF ALICE MEYNELL'S POEMS, GIVEN ME, YEARS AGO, BY A FRIEND

Upon this greying page you wrote
A whispered greeting, long ago.
Faint pencil-marks run to and fro
Scoring the lines I loved to quote.

A sea-shore of white, shoaling sand,
Blue creeks zigzagging through marsh-grasses,
Sand pipers, and a wind which passes
Cloudily silent up the land.

Upon the high edge of the sea
A great four-master sleeps; three hours
Her bowsprit has not cleared those flowers.
I read and look alternately.

It all comes back again, but dim
As pictures on a winking wall,
Hidden save when the dark clouds fall
Or crack to show the moon's bright rim.

I well remember what I was,
And what I wanted. You, unwise
With sore unwisdom, had no eyes
For what was patently the cause.

So are we sport of others' blindness,
We who could see right well alone.
What were you made of—wood or stone?
Yet I remember you with kindness.

You gave this book to me to ease
The smart in me you could not heal.
Your gift a mirror—woe or weal.
We sat beneath the apple-trees.

And I remember how they rang,
These words, like bronze cathedral bells
Down ancient lawns, or citadels
Thundering with gongs where choirs sang.

Silent the sea, the earth, the sky,
And in my heart a silent weeping.
Who has not sown can know no reaping!
Bitter conclusion and no lie.

O heart that sorrows, heart that bleeds,
Heart that was never mine, your words
Were like the pecking autumn birds
Stealing away my garnered seeds.

No future where there is no past!
O cherishing grief which laid me bare,
I wrapped you like a wintry air
About me. Poor enthusiast!

How strange that tumult, looking back.
The ink is pale, the letters fade.
The verses seem to be well made,
But I have lived the almanac.

And you are dead these drifted years,
How many I forget. And she

Who wrote the book, her tragedy
Long since dried up its scalding tears.

I read of her death yesterday,
Frail lady whom I never knew
And knew so well. Would I could strew
Her grave with pansies, blue and grey.

Would I could stand a little space
Under a blowing, brightening sky,
And watch the sad leaves fall and lie
Gently upon that lonely place.

So cried her heart, a feverish thing.
But clay is still, and clay is cold,
And I was young, and I am old,
And in December what birds sing!

Go, wistful book, go back again
Upon your shelf and gather dust.
I've seen the glitter through the rust
Of old, long years, I've known the pain.

I've recollected both of you,
But I shall recollect no more.
Between us I must shut the door.
The living have so much to do.

*The Atlantic Monthly,* March 1926


## THE SISTERS

Taking us by and large, we're a queer lot
We women who write poetry. And when you think
How few of us there've been, it's queerer still.
I wonder what it is that makes us do it,
Singles us out to scribble down, man-wise,

The fragments of ourselves. Why are we
Already mother-creatures, double-bearing,
With matrices in body and in brain?
I rather think that there is just the reason
We are so sparse a kind of human being;
The strength of forty thousand Atlases
Is needed for our every-day concerns.
There's Sappho, now I wonder what was Sappho.
I know a single slender thing about her:
That, loving, she was like a burning birch-tree
All tall and glittering fire, and that she wrote
Like the same fire caught up to Heaven and held there,
A frozen blaze before it broke and fell.
Ah, me! I wish I could have talked to Sappho,
Surprised her reticences by flinging mine
Into the wind. This tossing off of garments
Which cloud the soul is none too easy doing
With us to-day. But still I think with Sappho
One might accomplish it were she in the mood
To bare her loveliness of words and tell
The reasons, as she possibly conceived them,
Of why they are so lovely. Just to know
How she came at them, just to watch
The crisp sea sunshine playing on her hair,
And listen, thinking all the while 'twas she
Who spoke and that we two were sisters
Of a strange, isolated little family.
And she is Sappho—Sappho—not Miss or Mrs.,
A leaping fire we call so for convenience;
But Mrs. Browning—who would ever think
Of such presumption as to call her " Ba."
Which draws the perfect line between sea-cliffs
And a close-shuttered room in Wimpole Street.
Sappho could fly her impulses like bright
Balloons tip-tilting to a morning air
And write about it. Mrs. Browning's heart
Was squeezed in stiff conventions. So she lay

Stretched out upon a sofa, reading Greek
And speculating, as I must suppose,
In just this way on Sappho; all the need,
The huge, imperious need of loving, crushed
Within the body she believed so sick.
And it was sick, poor lady, because words
Are merely simulacra after deeds
Have wrought a pattern; when they take the place
Of actions they breed a poisonous miasma
Which, though it leave the brain, eats up the body.
So Mrs. Browning, aloof and delicate,
Lay still upon her sofa, all her strength
Going to uphold her over-topping brain.
It seems miraculous, but she escaped
To freedom and another motherhood
Than that of poems. She was a very woman
And needed both.
           If I had gone to call,
Would Wimpole Street have been the kindlier place,
Or Casa Guidi, in which to have met her?
I am a little doubtful of that meeting,
For Queen Victoria was very young and strong
And all-pervading in her apogee
At just that time. If we had stuck to poetry,
Sternly refusing to be drawn off by mesmerism
Or Roman revolutions, it might have done.
For, after all, she is another sister,
But always, I rather think, an older sister
And not herself so curious a technician
As to admit newfangled modes of writing—
"Except, of course, in Robert, and that is neither
Here nor there for Robert is a genius."
I do not like the turn this dream is taking,
Since I am very fond of Mrs. Browning
And very much indeed should like to hear her
Graciously asking me to call her "Ba."
But then the Devil of Verisimilitude

Creeps in and forces me to know she wouldn't.
Convention again, and how it chafes my nerves,
For we are such a little family
Of singing sisters, and as if I didn't know
What those years felt like tied down to the sofa.
Confound Victoria, and the slimy inhibitions
She loosed on all us Anglo-Saxon creatures!
Suppose there hadn't been a Robert Browning,
No "Sonnets from the Portuguese" would have been written.
They are the first of all her poems to be,
One might say, fertilized. For, after all,
A poet is flesh and blood as well as brain
And Mrs. Browning, as I said before,
Was very, very woman. Well, there are two
Of us, and vastly unlike that's for certain.
Unlike at least until we tear the veils
Away which commonly gird souls. I scarcely think
Mrs. Browning would have approved the process
In spite of what had surely been relief;
For speaking souls must always want to speak
Even when bat-eyed, narrow-minded Queens
Set prudishness to keep the keys of impulse.
Then do the frowning Gods invent new banes
And make the need of sofas. But Sappho was dead
And I, and others, not yet peeped above
The edge of possibility. So that's an end
To speculating over tea-time talks
Beyond the movement of pentameters
With Mrs. Browning.
                              But I go dreaming on,
In love with these my spiritual relations.
I rather think I see myself walk up
A flight of wooden steps and ring a bell
And send a card in to Miss Dickinson.
Yet that's a very silly way to do.
I should have taken the dream twist-ends about
And climbed over the fence and found her deep

Engrossed in the doings of a humming-bird
Among nasturtiums. Not having expected strangers,
She might forget to think me one, and holding up
A finger say quite casually: "Take care.
Don't frighten him, he's only just begun."
"Now this," I well believe I should have thought,
"Is even better than Sappho. With Emily
You're really here, or never anywhere at all
In range of mind." Wherefore, having begun
In the strict centre, we could slowly progress
To various circumferences, as we pleased.
We could, but should we? That would quite depend
On Emily. I think she'd be exacting,
Without intention possibly, and ask
A thousand tight-rope tricks of understanding.
But, bless you, I would somersault all day
If by so doing I might stay with her.
I hardly think that we should mention souls
Although they might just round the corner from us
In some half-quizzical, half-wistful metaphor.
I'm very sure that I should never seek
To turn her parables to stated fact.
Sappho would speak, I think, quite openly,
And Mrs. Browning guard a careful silence,
But Emily would set doors ajar and slam them
And love you for your speed of observation.

Strange trio of my sisters, most diverse;
And how extraordinarily unlike
Each is to me, and which way shall I go?
Sappho spent and gained; and Mrs. Browning,
After a miser girlhood, cut the strings
Which tied her money-bags and let them run;
But Emily hoarded—hoarded—only giving
Herself to cold, white paper. Starved and tortured,
She cheated her despair with games of patience
And fooled herself by winning. Frail little elf,

The lonely brain-child of a gaunt maturity,
She hung her womanhood upon a bough
And played ball with the stars—too long—too long—
The garment of herself hung on a tree
Until at last she lost even the desire
To take it down. Whose fault? Why let us say,
To be consistent, Queen Victoria's.
But really, not to over-rate the Queen,
I feel obliged to mention Martin Luther,
And behind him the long line of Church Fathers
Who draped their prurience like a dirty cloth
About the naked majesty of God.
Good-bye, my sisters, all of you are great,
And all of you are marvellously strange,
And none of you has any word for me.
I cannot write like you, I cannot think
In terms of Pagan or of Christian now.
I only hope that possibly some day
Some other woman with an itch for writing
May turn to me as I have turned to you
And chat with me a brief few minutes. How
We lie, we poets! It is three good hours
I have been dreaming. Has it seemed so long
To you? And yet I thank you for the time
Although you leave me sad and self-distrustful,
For older sisters are very sobering things.
Put on your cloaks, my dears, the motor's waiting.
No, you have not seemed strange to me, but near,
Frightfully near, and rather terrifying.
I understand you all, for in myself—
Is that presumption? Yet indeed it's true—
We are one family. And still my answer
Will not be any one of yours, I see.
Well, never mind that now. Good night! Good night!

# ADAPTED ASIAN FORMS
# AND TRANSLATIONS
# FROM THE CHINESE

> To be introduced to a new and magnificent literature, not
> through the medium of the usual more or less accurate translation,
> but directly, as one might burrow it out for one's self with the aid
> of a dictionary, is an exciting and inspiring thing. . . . I hold that
> it is more important to reproduce the perfume of a poem than its
> metrical from, and no translation can possibly reproduce both.
>
> —Amy Lowell, preface to *Fir-Flower Tablets*

## ALIENS

The chatter of little people
Breaks on my purpose
Like the water-drops which slowly wear the rocks to powder.
And while I laugh
My spirit crumbles at their teasing touch.

*Poetry,* September 1915

## THE POND

Cold, wet leaves
Floating on moss-coloured water
And the croaking of frogs—
Cracked bell-notes in the twilight.

*Poetry,* March 1916

## A LOVER

If I could catch the green lantern of the firefly
I could see to write you a letter.

*Poetry,* March 1917

## TO A HUSBAND

Brighter than fireflies upon the Uji River
Are your words in the dark, Beloved.

*Poetry,* March 1917

## A YEAR PASSES

Beyond the porcelain fence of the pleasure garden,
I hear the frogs in the blue-green ricefields;
But the sword-shaped moon
Has cut my heart in two.

*Poetry,* March 1917

## EPHEMERA

Silver-green lanterns tossing among windy branches:
So an old man thinks
Of the loves of his youth.

*Poetry,* March 1917

## AUTUMN

All day I have watched the purple vine-leaves
Fall into the water.
And now in the moonlight they still fall,
But each leaf is fringed with silver.

*Poetry,* March 1917

## ONE OF THE "HUNDRED VIEWS OF FUJI" BY HOKUSAI

Being thirsty,
I filled a cup with water,
And, behold!—Fuji-yama lay upon the water,
Like a dropped leaf!

*Poetry,* March 1917

## THE FISHERMAN'S WIFE

When I am alone,
The wind in the pine trees
Is like the shuffling of waves
Upon the wooden sides of a boat.

*Some Imagist Poets,* April 1917

## OUTSIDE A GATE

On the floor of the empty palaquin
The plum-petals constantly increase.

*Seven Arts,* October 1917

## IN TIME OF WAR

Across the newly-plastered wall,
The darting of red dragonflies
Is like the shooting
Of blood-tipped arrows.

*Youth,* October 1918

## LI T'AI-PO

So, Master, the wine gave you something,
I suppose.

I think I see you,
Your silks all disarranged,
Lolling in a green-marble pavilion,
Ogling the concubines of the Emperor's Court
Who pass the door
In yellow coats, and white jade ear-drops,
Their hair pleated in folds like the hundred clouds.
I watch you,
Hiccoughing poetry between drinks,
Sinking as the sun sinks,
Sleeping for twenty-four hours,
While they peek at you,
Giggling,
Through the open door.

You found something in the wine,
I imagine,
Since you could not leave it,
Even when, after years of wandering,
You sat in the boat with one sail,
Travelling down the zigzag rivers
On your way back to Court.

You had a dream,
I conjecture.
You saw something under the willow-lights of the water
Which swept you to dizziness,
So that you toppled over the edge of the boat,
And gasped, and became your dream.

Twelve hundred years
Or thereabouts.
Did the wine do it?
I would sit in the purple moonlight
And drink three hundred cups,
If I believed it.
Three hundred full cups,
After your excellent fashion,

While in front of me
The river dazzle ran before the moon,
And the light flaws of the evening wind
Scattered the notes of nightingales
Loosely among the kuai trees.

They erected a temple to you:
"Great Doctor,
Prince of Poetry,
Immortal man who loved drink."

I detest wine,
And I have no desire for the temple,
Which under the circumstances
Is fortunate.
But I would sacrifice even sobriety
If, when I was thoroughly drunk,
I could see what you saw
Under the willow-clouded water,
The day you died.

The Dial, September 1919

## FROSTY EVENING

It is not the bright light in your window
Which dazzles my eyes;
It is the dim outline of your shadow
Moving upon the shōji.

The Touchstone, September 1919

## A POET'S WIFE

CHO WĔN-CHŪN TO HER HUSBAND SSŬ-MA HSIANG-JU

You have taken our love and turned it into coins of silver.
You sell the love poems you wrote for me,
And with the price of them you buy many cups of wine.

I beg that you remain dumb,
That you write no more poems.
For the wine does us both an injury,
And the words of your heart
Have become the common speech of the Emperor's
    concubines.

*The Century,* September 1919

## THE RETURN

Coming up from my boat
In haste to lighten your anxiety,
I saw, reflected in the circular metal mirror,
The face and hands of a woman
Arranging her hair.

*Pictures of the Floating World,* 1919

## NUANCE

Even the iris bends
When a butterfly lights upon it.

*Pictures of the Floating World,* September 1919

## AUTUMN HAZE

Is it a dragonfly or a maple leaf
That settles softly down upon the water?

*Pictures of the Floating World,* September 1919

## NUIT BLANCHE

The chirping of crickets in the night
Is intermittent,
Like the twinkling of stars.

*Pictures of the Floating World,* September 1919

## AGAIN THE NEW YEAR'S FESTIVAL

I have drunk your health
In the red-lacquer wine cups,
But the wind-bells on the bronze lanterns
In my garden
Are corroded and fallen.

*Pictures of the Floating World*, September 1919

## TIME

Looking at myself in my metal mirror,
I saw, faintly outlined,
The figure of a crane
Engraved upon its back.

*Pictures of the Floating World*, September 1919

## NOSTALGIA

"Through pleasures and palaces"—
Through hotels, and Pullman cars, and steamships . . .

Pink and white camellias floating in a crystal bowl,
The sharp smell of firewood,
The scrape and rustle of a dog stretching himself on a
    hardwood floor,
And your voice, reading—reading—to the slow ticking of an
    old brass clock . . .

"Tickets, please!"
And I watch the man in front of me
Fumbling in fourteen pockets,
While the conductor balances his ticket-punch
Between his fingers.

*Pictures of the Floating World*, September 1919

## AFTERGLOW

Peonies
The strange pink colour of Chinese porcelains;
Wonderful—the glow of them.
But, my Dear, it is the pale blue larkspur
Which swings windily against my heart.
Other summers—
And a cricket chirping in the grass.

*The Bookman,* April 1921

## VESPERS

Last night, at sunset,
The foxgloves were like tall altar candles.
Could I have lifted you to the roof of the greenhouse, my
    Dear,
I should have understood their burning.

*American Poetry,* 1922

## THE BATTLE TO THE SOUTH OF THE CITY

*Li T'ai-po*

How dim the battle-field as yellow dusk!
The fighting men are like a swarm of ants
The air is thick, the sun a red wheel.
Blood dyes the wild chrysanthemums purple.
Vultures hold the flesh of men in their mouths,
They are heavy with food—they cannot rise to fly.
There were men yesterday on the city wall;
There are ghosts to-day below the city wall.
Colours of flags like a net of stars,
Rolling of horse-carried drums—not yet is the killing ended.
From the house of the Unworthy One—a husband, sons.
All within earshot of the rolling horse-drums.

*North American Review,* July 1921

## THE RETREAT OF HSIEH KUNG

*Li T'ai-po*

The sun is setting—has set—on the Spring-green Mountain.
Hsieh Kung's retreat is solitary and still.
No sound of man in the bamboo grove.
The white moon shines in the centre of the unused garden
  pool.
All round the ruined Summer-house is decaying grass,
Grey mosses choke the abandoned well.
There is only the free, clear wind
Again—again—passing over the stones of the spring.

*The Dial*, October 1921

## THE TERRACED ROAD OF THE
## TWO-EDGED SWORD MOUNTAINS

*Li T'ai-po*

Looking South and straight from Hsien Yang for five thou-
  sand *li,*
One could see, among the full, blowing clouds, the rocky
  sharpness of peaks,
Were it not for the horizontal line of the two-Edged Sword
  Mountains cutting across the view.
They are flat against the green sky, and open in the middle to
  let the sky through.
On their heights, the wind whistles awesomely in the pines; it
  booms in great, long gusts; it clashes like the strings of a
  jade-stone psaltery; it shouts on the clearness of a gale.
In the Serpent River country, the gibbons—Oh-h-h-h-h—
  all the gibbons together moan and grieve.
Beside the road, torrents flung from a great height rush down
  the gully,
They toss stones and spray over the road, they run rapidly,
  they whirl, they startle with the noise of thunder.
I bid good-bye to my devoted friend—Oh-h-h-h-h—now
  he leaves me.

When will he come again? Oh-h-h-h-h—When will he
   return to me?
I hope for my dear friend the utmost peace.
My voice is heavy, I sigh and draw my breath haltingly.
I look at the green surface of the water flowing to the East.
I grieve that the white sun hides in the West.
The wild goose has taken the place of the swallow.—
   Oh-h-h-h-h—I hear the pattering, falling noises of
   Autumn.
Dark are the rain clouds; the colour of the town of Chin is
   dark.
When the moon glistens on the Road of the Two-Edged
   Sword—Oh-h-h-h-h—
I and you, even though in different provinces, may drink our
   wine opposite each other.
And listen to the talking
Of our hearts.

Asia: The American Magazine on the Orient, October 1921

## LOOKING AT THE MOON AFTER RAIN

Li T'ai-po

The heavy clouds are broken and blowing,
And once more I can see the wide common stretching beyond
   the four sides of the city.
Open the door. Half of the moon-toad is already up,
The glimmer of it is like smooth hoarfrost spreading over
   ten thousand *li.*
The river is a flat, shining chain.
The moon, rising, is a white eye to the hills;
After it has risen, it is the bright heart of the sea.
Because I love it—so—round as a fan,
I hum songs until the dawn.

Fir-Flower Tablets, December 1921

## THE LONELY WIFE

*Li T'ai-po*

The mist is thick. On the wide river, the water-plants float
    smoothly.
No letters come; none go.
There is only the moon, shining through the clouds of a hard,
    jade-green sky,
Looking down at us so far divided, so anxiously apart.
All day, going about my affairs, I suffer and grieve, and press
    the thought of you closely to my heart.
My eyebrows are locked in sorrow, I cannot separate them.
Nightly, nightly, I keep ready half the quilt,
And wait for the return of that divine dream which is my
    Lord.

Beneath the quilt of the Fire-Bird, on the bed of the
    Silver-Crested Love-Pheasant,
Nightly, nightly, I drowse alone.
The red candles in the silver candlesticks melt, and the wax
    runs from them,
As the tears of your so Unworthy One escape and continue
    constantly to flow.
A flower face endures but a short season,
Yet still he drifts along the river Hsiao and the river Hsiang.
As I toss on my pillow, I hear the cold nostalgic sound of the
    water-clock:
Shêng! Shêng! it drips, cutting my heart in two.

I rise at dawn. In the Hall of Pictures
They come and tell me that the snow-flowers are falling.
The reed-blind is rolled high, and I gaze at the beautiful,
    glittering, primeval snow,
Whitening the distance, confusing the stone steps and the
    courtyard.
The air is filled with its shining, it blows far out like the
    smoke of a furnace.

The grass-blades are cold and white, like jade girdle pendants.
Surely the Immortals in Heaven must be crazy with wine to
    cause such disorder,
Seizing the white clouds, crumpling them up, destroying
    them.

*Fir-Flower Tablets,* December 1921

## ON HEARING THE BUDDHIST PRIEST
## OF SHU PLAY HIS TABLE-LUTE

*Li T'ai-po*

The Priest of the Province of Shu, carrying his table-lute in a
    cover of green, shot silk,
Comes down the Western slope of the peak of Mount Omei.
He moves his hands for me, striking the lute.
It is like listening to the water in ten thousand ravines, and the
    wind in ten thousand pine-trees.
The traveller's heart is washed clean as in flowing water.
The echoes of the overtones join with the evening bell.
I am not conscious of the sunset behind the jade-grey hill,
Nor how many and dark are the Autumn clouds.

*Fir-Flower Tablets,* December 1921

## PARROT ISLAND

*Li T'ai-po*

The parrots come, they cross the river waters of Wu.
The island in the river is called Parrot Island.
The parrots are flying West to the Dragon Mountain.
There are sweet grasses on the island, and how green, green,
    are its trees!

The mists part and one can see the leaves of the spear-orchid,
    and its scent is warm on the wind;
The water is embroidered and shot with the reflections of the
    peach-tree blossoms growing on both banks.

Now indeed does the departing official realize the full
  meaning of his banishment.
The long island—the solitary moon—facing each other in the
  brightness.

*Fir-Flower Tablets,* December 1921


## REPLY TO AN UNREFINED PERSON
## ENCOUNTERED IN THE HILLS

*Li T'ai-po*

He asks why I perch in the green jade hills.
I smile and do not answer. My heart is comfortable and
  at peace.
Fallen peach-flowers spread out widely, widely, over the
  water.
It is another sky and earth, not the world of man.

*Fir-Flower Tablets,* December 1921


## NIGHT THOUGHTS

*Li T'ai-po*

In front of my bed the moonlight is very bright.
I wonder if that can be frost on the floor?
I lift up my head and look full at the full moon, the dazzling
  moon.
I drop my head and think of the home of old days.

*Fir-Flower Tablets,* December 1921


## IN THE PROVINCE OF LU, TO THE EAST OF
## THE STONE GATE MOUNTAIN, TAKING LEAVE OF TU FU

*Li T'ai-po*

When drunk, we were divided; but we have been together
  again for several days.

We have climbed everywhere, to every pool and ledge.
When, on the Stone Gate Road,
Shall we pour from the golden flagon again?
The Autumn leaves drop into the Four Waters,
The Ch'u Mountain is brightly reflected in the colour of the
    lake.
We are flying like thistledown, each to a different distance;
Pending this, we drain the cups in our hands.

*Fir-Flower Tablets,* December 1921


## A POEM SENT TO TU FU FROM SHA CH'IU CH'ÊNG

*Li T'ai-po*


After all, what have I come here to do?
To lie and meditate at Sha Ch'iu Ch'êng.
Near the city are ancient trees,
And day and night are continuous with Autumn noises.
One cannot get drunk on Lu wine,
The songs of Ch'I have no power to excite emotion.
I think of my friend, and my thoughts are like the Wên River,
Mightily moving, directed toward the South.

*Fir-Flower Tablets,* December 1921


## THE RIVER VILLAGE

*Tu Fu*


The river makes a bend and encircles the village with its
    current.
All the long Summer, the affairs and the occupations of the
    river village are quiet and simple.
The swallows who nest in the beams go and come as they
    please.
The gulls in the middle of the river enjoy one another, they
    crowd together and touch one another.

My old wife paints a chess-board on paper.
My little sons hammer needles to make fish-hooks.
I have many illnesses, therefore my only necessities are
    medicines;
Besides these, what more can so humble a man as I ask?

*Fir-Flower Tablets*, December 1921

## THE SORCERESS GORGE

*Tu Fu*

Jade dew lies upon the withered and wounded forest of
    maple-trees.
On the Sorceress Hill, over the Sorceress Gorge, the mist is
    desolate and dark.
The ripples of the river increase into waves and blur with the
    rapidly flowing sky.
The wind-clouds at the horizon become confused with the
    Earth. Darkness.
The myriad chrysanthemums have bloomed twice. Days to
    come—tears.
The solitary little boat is moored, but my heart is in the
    old-time garden.
Everywhere people are hastening to measure and cut out their
    Winter clothes.
At sunset, in the high City of the White Emperor, the hurried
    pounding of washed garments.

*Fir-Flower Tablets*, December 1920

## AT THE EDGE OF HEAVEN, THINKING OF LI PO

*Tu Fu*

A cold wind blows up from the edge of Heaven.
The state of mind of the superior man is what?
When does the wild goose arrive?
Autumn water flows high in the rivers and lakes.

They hated your essay—yet your fate was to succeed.
The demons where you are rejoice to see men go by.
You should hold speech with the soul of Yüan,
And toss a poem into the Mi Lo River as a gift to him.

*Fir-Flower Tablets,* December 1921


## SENT TO LI PO AS A GIFT

*Tu Fu*


Autumn comes,
We meet each other.
You still whirl about as a thistledown in the wind.
Your Elixir of Immortality is not yet perfected
And, remembering Ko Hung, you are ashamed.
You drink a great deal,
You sing wild songs,
Your days pass in emptiness.
Your nature is a spreading fire,
It is swift and strenuous.
But what does all this bravery amount to?

*Fir-Flower Tablets,* December 1920


## A TOAST FOR MÊNG YÜN-CH'ING

*Tu Fu*


Illimitable happiness,
But grief for our white heads.
We love the long watches of the night, the red candle.
It would be difficult to have too much of meeting,
Let us now be in a hurry to talk of separation.

But because the Heaven River will sink,
We had better empty the wine-cups.
To-morrow, at bright dawn, the world's business will
    entangle us.
We brush away our tears,
We go—East and West.

*Fir-Flower Tablets,* December 1921


## THE BLUE-GREEN STREAM

*Wang Wei*


Every time I have started for the Yellow Flower River,
I have gone down the Blue-Green Stream,
Following the hills, making ten thousand turnings.
We go along rapidly, but advance scarcely one hundred *li.*
We are in the midst of a noise of water,
Of the confused and mingled sounds of water broken by
    stones,
And in the deep darkness of pine-trees.
Rocked, rocked,
Moving on and on,
We float past water-chestnuts
Into a still clearness reflecting reeds and rushes.
My heart is clean and white as silk; it has already achieved
    Peace;
It is smooth as the placid river.
I long to stay here, curled up on the rocks,
Dropping my fish-line forever.

*Fir-Flower Tablets,* December 1921

## TOGETHER WE KNOW HAPPINESS
*Written by a descendant of the founder of the Southern T'ang Dynasty*

Silent and alone, I ascended the West Cupola.
The moon was like a golden hook.
In the quiet, empty, inner courtyard, the coolness of early
    Autumn enveloped the wu-t'ung tree.
Scissors cannot cut this thing;
Unravelled, it joins again and clings.
It is the sorrow of separation,
And none other tastes to the heart like this.

*Fir-Flower Tablets,* December 1921

# CADENCED
# VERSE

They are built upon "organic rhythm," or the rhythm of the speaking voice with its necessity for breathing, rather than upon a strict metrical system. They differ from ordinary prose rhythms by being more curved, and containing more stress.

—AMY LOWELL, preface to
*Sword Blades and Poppy Seeds*

## IN A GARDEN

Gushing from the mouths of stone men
To spread at ease under the sky
In granite-lipped basins,
Where iris dabble their feet
And rustle to a passing wind,
The water fills the garden with its rushing,
In the midst of the quiet of close-clipped lawns.

Damp smell the ferns in tunnels of stone,
Where trickle and plash the fountains,
Marble fountains, yellowed with much water.

Splashing down moss-tarnished steps
It falls, the water;
And the air is throbbing with it;
With its gurgling and running;
With its leaping, and deep, cool murmur.

And I wished for night and you.
I wanted to see you in the swimming-pool,
White and shining in the silver-flecked water.

While the moon rode over the garden,
High in the arch of night,
And the scent of the lilacs was heavy with stillness.

Night and the water, and you in your whiteness, bathing!

*The New Freewoman: An Individualist Review,* September 1912

## ABSENCE

My cup is empty to-night,
Cold and dry are its sides,
Chilled by the wind from the open window.
Empty and void, it sparkles white in the moonlight.
The room is filled with the strange scent
Of wistaria blossoms.
They sway in the moon's radiance
And tap against the wall.
But the cup of my heart is still,
And cold, and empty.

When you come, it brims
Red and trembling with blood,
Heart's blood for your drinking;
To fill your mouth with love
And the bitter-sweet taste of a soul.

*The Atlantic Monthly,* November 1913


## AUBADE

As I would free the white almond from the green husk
So would I strip your trappings off,
Beloved.
And fingering the smooth and polished kernel
I should see that in my hands glittered a gem beyond
    counting.

*The Egoist,* February 1914


## WHITE AND GREEN

Hey! My daffodil-crowned,
Slim and without sandals!

As the sudden spurt of flame upon darkness
So my eyeballs are startled with you,
Supple-limbed youth among the fruit-trees,
Light runner through tasselled orchards.
You are an almond flower unsheathed
Leaping and flickering between the budded branches.

*The Egoist,* February 1914


## THE CAPTURED GODDESS

Over the housetops,
Above the rotating chimney-pots,
I have seen a shiver of amethyst,
And blue and cinnamon have flickered,
A moment,
At the far end of a dusty street.

Through sheeted rain
Has come a lustre of crimson,
And I have watched moonbeams
Hushed by a film of palest green.

It was her wings,
Goddess!
Who stepped over the clouds,
And laid her rainbow feathers
Aslant, on the currents of the air.

I followed her for long,
With gazing eyes and stumbling feet.
I cared not where she led me,
My eyes were full of colours:
Saffrons, rubies, the yellows of beryls,
And the indigo-blue of quartz;
Flights of rose, layers of chrysoprase,

Points of orange, spirals of vermilion,
The spotted gold of tiger-lily petals,
The loud pink of bursting hydrangeas.
I followed,
And watched for the flashing of her wings.

In the city I found her,
The narrow-streeted city.
In the market-place I came upon her,
Bound and trembling.
Her fluted wings were fastened to her sides with cords,
She was naked and cold,
For that day the wind blew
Without sunshine.

Men chaffered for her,
They bargained in silver and gold,
In copper, in wheat,
And called their bids across the market-place.

The Goddess wept.

Hiding my face I fled,
And the grey wind hissed behind me,
Along the narrow streets.

*The Egoist*, February 1914


## THE TAXI

When I go away from you
The world beats dead
Like a slackened drum.
I call out for you against the jutted stars
And shout into the ridges of the wind.
Streets coming fast,
One after the other,
Wedge you away from me,

And the lamps of the city prick my eyes
So that I can no longer see your face.
Why should I leave you,
To wound myself upon the sharp edges of the night?

*The Egoist,* August 1914

## THE BLUE SCARF

Pale, with the blue of high zeniths, shimmered over with
    silver, brocaded
In smooth, running patterns, a soft stuff, with dark knotted
    fringes, it lies there,
Warm from a woman's soft shoulders, and my fingers close on
    it, caressing.
Where is she, the woman who wore it? The scent of her
    lingers and drugs me.
A languor, fire-shotted, runs through me, and I crush the
    scarf down on my face,
And gulp in the warmth and the blueness, and my eyes swim
    in cool-tinted heavens.
Around me are columns of marble, and a diapered,
    sun-flickered pavement.
Rose-leaves blow and patter against it. Below the stone steps
    a lute tinkles.
A jar of green jade throws its shadow half over the floor. A
    big-bellied
Frog hops through the sunlight, and plops in the
    gold-bubbled water of a basin,
Sunk in the black and white marble. The west wind has lifted
    a scarf
On the seat close beside me; the blue of it is a violent outrage
    of colour.
She draws it more closely about her, and it ripples beneath
    her slight stirring.
Her kisses are sharp buds of fire; and I burn back against her,
    a jewel

Hard and white, a stalked, flaming flower; till I break to a
   handful of cinders,
And open my eyes to the scarf, shining blue in the afternoon
   sunshine.

How loud clocks can tick when a room is empty, and one is
   alone!

*The Century,* August 1914


## THE LETTER

Little cramped words scrawling all over the paper
Like draggled fly's legs,
What can you tell of the flaring moon
Through the oak leaves?
Or of my uncurtained window and the bare floor
Spattered with moonlight?
Your silly quirks and twists have nothing in them
Of blossoming hawthorns,
And this paper is dull, crisp, smooth, virgin of loveliness
Beneath my hand.

I am tired, Beloved, of chafing my heart against
The want of you;
Of squeezing it into little inkdrops,
And posting it.
And I scald alone, here, under the fire
Of the great moon.

*Poetry and Drama,* September 1914


## PINE, BEECH, AND SUNLIGHT

The sudden April heat
Stretches itself
Under the smooth, leafless branches

Of the beech-tree,
And lies lightly
Upon the great patches
Of purple and white crocus
With their panting, wide-open cups.

A clear wind
Slips through the naked beech boughs,
And their shadows scarcely stir.
But the pine-trees beyond sigh
When it passes over them
And presses back their needles,
And slides gently down their stems.

It is a languor of pale, south-starting sunlight
Come upon a morning unawaked,
And holding her drowsing.

*Poetry and Drama*, September 1914

## ASTIGMATISM

*To Ezra Pound*
*with Much Friendship and Admiration*
*and Some Differences of Opinion*

The Poet took his walking-stick
Of fine and polished ebony.
Set in the close-grained wood
Were quaint devices;
Patterns in ambers,
And in the clouded green of jades.
The top was of smooth, yellow ivory,
And a tassel of tarnished gold
Hung by a faded cord from a hole
Pierced in the hard wood,
Circled with silver.
For years the Poet had wrought upon this cane.

His wealth had gone to enrich it,
His experiences to pattern it,
His labour to fashion and burnish it.
To him it was perfect,
A work of art and a weapon,
A delight and a defence.
The Poet took his walking-stick
And walked abroad.

Peace be with you, Brother.

The Poet came to a meadow.
Sifted through the grass were daisies,
Open-mouthed, wondering, they gazed at the sun.
The Poet struck them with his cane.
The little heads flew off, and they lay
Dying, open-mouthed and wondering,
On the hard ground.
"They are useless. They are not roses," said the Poet.

Peace be with you, Brother. Go your ways.

The Poet came to a stream.
Purple and blue flags waded in the water;
In among them hopped the speckled frogs;
The wind slid through them, rustling.
The Poet lifted his cane,
And the iris heads fell into the water.
They floated away, torn and drowning.
"Wretched flowers," said the Poet,
"They are not roses."

Peace be with you, Brother. It is your affair.

The Poet came to a garden.
Dahlias ripened against a wall,
Gillyflowers stood up bravely for all their short stature,
And a trumpet-vine covered an arbour

With the red and gold of its blossoms.
Red and gold like the brass notes of trumpets.
The Poet knocked off the stiff heads of the dahlias,
And his cane lopped the gillyflowers at the ground.
Then he severed the trumpet-blossoms from their stems.
Red and gold they lay scattered,
Red and gold, as on a battle field;
Red and gold, prone and dying.
"They were not roses," said the Poet.

Peace be with you, Brother.
But behind you is destruction, and waste places.

The Poet came home at evening,
And in the candle-light
He wiped and polished his cane.
The orange candle flame leaped in the yellow ambers,
And made the jades undulate like green pools.
It played along the bright ebony,
And glowed in the top of cream-coloured ivory.
But these things were dead,
Only the candle-light made them seem to move.
"It is a pity there were no roses," said the Poet.

Peace be with you, Brother. You have chosen your part.

*Sword Blades and Poppy Seed,* September 1914

## THE GIVER OF STARS

Hold your soul open for my welcoming.
Let the quiet of your spirit bathe me
With its clear and rippled coolness,
That, loose-limbed and weary, I find rest,
Outstretched upon your peace, as on a bed of ivory.

Let the flickering flame of your soul play all about me,
That into my limbs may come the keenness of fire,

The life and joy of tongues of flame,
And, going out from you, tightly strung and in tune,
I may rouse the blear-eyed world,
And pour into it the beauty which you have begotten.

*Sword Blades and Poppy Seed,* September 1914

## BRIGHT SUNLIGHT

The wind has blown a corner of your shawl
Into the fountain,
Where it floats and drifts
Among the lily-pads
Like a tissue of sapphires.
But you do not heed it,
Your fingers pick at the lichens
On the stone edge of the basin,
And your eyes follow the tall clouds
As they sail over the ilex-trees.

*The Little Review,* August 1915

## VENUS TRANSIENS

Tell me,
Was Venus more beautiful
Than you are,
When she topped
The crinkled waves,
Drifting shoreward
On her plaited shell?
Was Botticelli's vision
Fairer than mine;
And were the painted rosebuds
He tossed his lady
Of better worth
Than the words I blow about you

To cover your too great loveliness
As with a gauze
Of misted silver?

For me,
You stand poised
In the blue and buoyant air,
Cinctured by bright winds,
Treading the sunlight.
And the waves which precede you
Ripple and stir
The sands at my feet.

*Poetry,* April 1915


## A RAINY NIGHT

Shadows,
And white, moving light,
And the snap and sparkle of rain on the window,
An electric lamp in the street
Is swinging, tossing,
Making the rain-runnelled window-glass
Glitter and palpitate.
In its silver lustre
I can see the old four-post bed,
With the fringes and balls of its canopy.
You are lying beside me, waiting,
But I do not turn,
I am counting the folds of the canopy.
You are lying beside me, waiting,
But I do not turn.
In the silver light you would be too beautiful,
And there are ten pleats on this side of the bed canopy,
And ten on the other.

*The Egoist,* July 1915

## PATTERNS

I walk down the garden paths,
And all the daffodils
Are blowing, and the bright blue squills.
I walk down the patterned garden paths
In my stiff, brocaded gown.
With my powdered hair and jewelled fan,
I too am a rare
Pattern. As I wander down
The garden paths.

My dress is richly figured,
And the train
Makes a pink and silver stain
On the gravel, and the thrift
Of the borders.
Just a plate of current fashion,
Tripping by in high-heeled, ribboned shoes.
Not a softness anywhere about me,
Only whale-bone and brocade.
And I sink on a seat in the shade
Of a lime tree. For my passion
Wars against the stiff brocade.
The daffodils and squills
Flutter in the breeze
As they please.
And I weep;
For the lime tree is in blossom
And one small flower has dropped upon my bosom.

And the splashing of waterdrops
In the marble fountain
Comes down the garden paths.
The dripping never stops.
Underneath my stiffened gown
Is the softness of a woman bathing in a marble basin,

A basin in the midst of hedges grown
So thick, she cannot see her lover hiding,
But she guesses he is near,
And the sliding of the water
Seems the stroking of a dear
Hand upon her.
What is Summer in a fine brocaded gown!
I should like to see it lying in a heap upon the ground.
All the pink and silver crumpled up on the ground.

I would be the pink and silver as I ran along the paths,
And he would stumble after,
Bewildered by my laughter.
I should see the sun flashing from his sword-hilt and the
    buckles on his shoes.
I would choose
To lead him in a maze along the patterned paths,
A bright and laughing maze for my heavy-booted lover,
Till he caught me in the shade,
And the buttons of his waistcoat bruised my body as he
    clasped me,
Aching, melting, unafraid.
With the shadows of the leaves and the sundrops,
And the plopping of the waterdrops,
All about us in the open afternoon—
I am very like to swoon
With the weight of this brocade,
For the sun sifts through the shade.

Underneath the fallen blossom
In my bosom,
Is a letter I have hid.
It was brought to me this morning by a rider from the Duke.
"Madam, we regret to inform you that Lord Hartwell
Died in action Thursday sen'night."
As I read it in the white, morning sunlight,
The letters squirmed like snakes.

"Any answer, Madam," said my footman.
"No," I told him.
"See that the messenger takes some refreshment.
No, no answer."
And I walked into the garden,
Up and down the patterned paths,
In my stiff, correct brocade.
The blue and yellow flowers stood up proudly in the sun,
Each one.
I stood upright too,
Held rigid to the pattern
By the stiffness of my gown.
Up and down I walked,
Up and down.

In a month he would have been my husband.
In a month, here, underneath this lime,
We would have broke the pattern;
He for me, and I for him,
He as Colonel, I as Lady,
On this shady seat.
He had a whim
That sunlight carried blessing.
And I answered, "It shall be as you have said."
Now he is dead.

In Summer and in Winter I shall walk
Up and down
The patterned garden paths
In my stiff, brocaded gown.
The squills and daffodils
Will give place to pillared roses, and to asters, and to snow.
I shall go
Up and down,
In my gown.
Gorgeously arrayed,
Boned and stayed.

And the softness of my body will be guarded from embrace
By each button, hook, and lace.
For the man who should loose me is dead,
Fighting with the Duke in Flanders,
In a pattern called a war.
Christ! What are patterns for?

*The Little Review*, August 1915

## STRAIN

It is late
And the clock is striking thin hours,
But sleep has become a terror to me,
Lest I wake in the night
Bewildered,
And stretching out my arms to comfort myself with you,
Clasp instead the cold body of the darkness.
All night it will hunger over me,
And push and undulate against me,
Breathing into my mouth
And passing long fingers through my drifting hair.
Only the dawn can loose me from it,
And the grey streaks of morning melt it from my side.
Bring many candles,
Though they stab my tired brain
And hurt it.
For I am afraid of the twining of the darkness
And dare not sleep.

*Poetry*, September 1915

## FROM STRAVINSKY'S THREE PIECES "GROTESQUES," FOR STRING QUARTET, SECOND MOVEMENT

Pale violin music whiffs across the moon,
A pale smoke of violin music blows over the moon,

Cherry petals fall and flutter,
And the white Pierrot,
Wreathed in the smoke of the violins,
Splashed with cherry petals falling, falling,
Claws a grave for himself in the fresh earth
With his finger-nails.

*The Little Review*, March 1916

## SUMMER RAIN

All night our room was outer-walled with rain.
Drops fell and flattened on the tin roof,
And rang like little disks of metal.
Ping!—Ping!—and there was not a pin-point of silence
     between them.
The rain rattled and clashed,
And the slats of the shutters danced and glittered.
But to me the darkness was red-gold and crocus-coloured
With your brightness,
And the words you whispered to me
Sprang up and flamed—orange torches against the rain.
Torches against the wall of cool, silver rain!

*Smart Set*, April 1916

## A DECADE

When you came you were like red wine and honey,
And the taste of you burnt my mouth with its sweetness.
Now you are like morning bread—
Smooth and pleasant.
I hardly taste you at all for I know your savour,
But I am completely nourished.

*Chimera*, May 1916

## AN AQUARIUM

Streaks of green and yellow iridescence,
Silver shiftings,
Rings veering out of rings,
Silver—gold—
Grey-green opaqueness sliding down,
With sharp white bubbles
Shooting and dancing,
Flinging quickly outward.
Nosing the bubbles,
Swallowing them,
Fish.
Blue shadows against silver-saffron water,
The light rippling over them
In steel-bright tremors.
Outspread translucent fins
Flute, fold, and relapse;
The threaded light prints through them on the pebbles
In scarcely tarnished twinklings.
Curving of spotted spines,
Slow up-shifts,
Lazy convolutions:
Then a sudden swift straightening
And darting below:
Oblique grey shadows
Athwart a pale casement.
Roped and curled,
Green man-eating eels
Slumber in undulate rhythms,
With crests laid horizontal on their backs.
Barred fish,
Striped fish,
Uneven disks of fish,
Slip, slide, whirl, turn,
And never touch.

Metallic blue fish,
With fins wide and yellow and swaying
Like Oriental fans,
Hold the sun in their bellies
And glow with light:
Blue brilliance cut by black bars.
An oblong pane of straw-coloured shimmer,
Across it, in a tangent,
A smear of rose, black, silver.
Short twists and upstartings,
Rose-black, in a setting of bubbles:
Sunshine playing between red and black flowers
On a blue and gold lawn.
Shadows and polished surfaces,
Facets of mauve and purple,
A constant modulation of values.
Shaft-shaped,
With green bead eyes;
Thick-nosed,
Heliotrope-coloured;
Swift spots of chrysolite and coral;
In the midst of green, pearl, amethyst irradiations.

Outside,
A willow-tree flickers
With little white jerks,
And long blue waves
Rise steadily beyond the outer islands.

*Reedy's Mirror,* July 1916


## THOMPSON'S LUNCH ROOM—GRAND CENTRAL STATION

*STUDY IN WHITES*
Wax-white—
Floor, ceiling, walls.
Ivory shadows

Over the pavement
Polished to cream surfaces
By constant sweeping.
The big room is coloured like the petals
Of a great magnolia,
And has a patina
Of flower bloom
Which makes it shine dimly
Under the electric lamps.
Chairs are ranged in rows
Like sepia seeds
Waiting fulfilment.
The chalk-white spot of a cook's cap
Moves unglossily against the vaguely bright wall—
Dull chalk-white striking the retina like a blow
Thru the wavering uncertainty of steam.
Vitreous-white of glasses with green reflections,
Ice-green carboys, shifting—greener, bluer—with the jar of
    moving water.
Jagged green-white bowls of pressed glass
Rearing snow-peaks of chipped sugar
Above the lighthouse-shaped castors
Of grey pepper and grey-white salt.
Grey-white placards: "Oyster Stew, Cornbeef Hash,
    Frankfurters":
Marble slabs veined with words in meandering lines.
Dropping on the white counter like horn notes
Through a web of violins,
The flat yellow lights of oranges,
The cube-red splashes of apples,
In high plated *épergnes*.
The electric clock jerks every half-minute:
"Coming!—Past!"
"Three beef-steaks and a chicken-pie,"
Bawled through a slide while the clock jerks heavily.
A man carries a china mug of coffee to a distant chair.
Two rice puddings and a salmon salad

Are pushed over the counter;
The unfulfilled chairs open to receive them.
A spoon falls upon the floor with the impact of metal striking
    stone,
And the sound throws across the room
Sharp, invisible zigzags
Of silver.

*The Independent,* August 1916


## OPAL

You are ice and fire,
The touch of you burns my hands like snow.
You are cold and flame.
You are the crimson of amaryllis,
The silver of moon-touched magnolias.
When I am with you,
My heart is a frozen pond
Gleaming with agitated torches.

*The Independent,* August 1916


## MISE EN SCÈNE

When I think of you, Beloved,
I see a smooth and stately garden
With parterres of gold and crimson tulips
And bursting lilac leaves.
There is a low-lipped basin in the midst,
Where a statue of veined cream marble
Perpetually pours water over her shoulder
From a tilted urn.
When the wind blows,
The water-stream blows before it
And spatters into the basin with a light tinkling,

And your shawl—the colour of red violets—
Flares out behind you in great curves
Like the swirling draperies of a painted Madonna.

*The Independent,* August 1916


## WAKEFULNESS

Jolt of market-carts;
Steady drip of horses' hoofs on hard pavement;
A black sky lacquered over with blueness,
And the lights of Battersea Bridge
Pricking pale in the dawn.
The beautiful hours are passing
And still you sleep!
Tired heart of my joy,
Incurved upon your dreams,
Will the day come before you have opened to me?

*The Little Review,* August 1916


## A BATHER

Thick dappled by circles of sunshine and fluttering shade,
Your bright, naked body advances, blown over by leaves,
Half-quenched in their various green, just a point of you
    showing,
A knee or a thigh, sudden glimpsed, then at once blotted into
The filmy and flickering forest, to start out again
Triumphant in smooth, supple roundness, edged sharp as
    white ivory,
Cool, perfect, with rose rarely tinting your lips and your
    breasts,
Swelling out from the green in the opulent curves of ripe fruit,
And hidden, like fruit, by the swift intermittence of leaves.
So, clinging to branches and moss, you advance on the ledges

Of rock which hang over the stream, with the wood-smells
    about you,
The pungence of strawberry plants, and of gum-oozing
    spruces,
While below runs the water impatient, impatient—to
    take you,
To splash you, to run down your sides, to sing you of
    deepness,
Of pools brown and golden, with brown-and-gold flags on
    their borders,
Of blue, lingering skies floating solemnly over your beauty,
Of undulant waters a-sway in the effort to hold you,
To keep you submerged and quiescent while over you glories
The summer.

    Oread, Dryad, or Naiad, or just
Woman, clad only in youth and in gallant perfection,
Standing up in a great burst of sunshine, you dazzle my eyes
Like a snow-star, a moon, your effulgence burns up in a halo,
For you are the chalice which holds all the races of men.

You slip into the pool and the water folds over your shoulder
And over the tree-tops the clouds slowly follow your
    swimming,
And the scent of the woods is sweet on this hot summer
    morning.

*Harper's,* August 1917

## MADONNA OF THE EVENING FLOWERS

All day long I have been working,
Now I am tired.
I call: "Where are you?"
But there is only the oak tree rustling in the wind.
The house is very quiet,
The sun shines in on your books,

On your scissors and thimble just put down,
But you are not there.
Suddenly I am lonely:
Where are you?
I go about searching.

Then I see you,
Standing under a spire of pale blue larkspur,
With a basket of roses on your arm.
You are cool, like silver,
And you smile.
I think the Canterbury bells are playing little tunes.

You tell me that the peonies need spraying,
That the columbines have overrun all bounds,
That the pyrus japonica should be cut back and rounded.
You tell me these things.
But I look at you, heart of silver,
White heart-flame of polished silver,
Burning beneath the blue steeples of the larkspur.
And I long to kneel instantly at your feet,
While all about us peal the loud, sweet *Te Deums* of the
    Canterbury bells.

*North American Review,* February 1918

## *FROM* DREAMS IN WAR TIME

I
I wandered through a house of many rooms.
It grew darker and darker,
Until, at last, I could only find my way
By passing my fingers along the wall.
Suddenly my hand shot through an open window,
And the thorn of a rose I could not see
Pricked it so sharply
That I cried aloud.

II

I dug a grave under an oak-tree.
With infinite care, I stamped my spade
Into the heavy grass.
The sod sucked it,
And I drew it out with effort,
Watching the steel run liquid in the moonlight
As it came clear.
I stooped, and dug, and never turned,
For behind me,
On the dried leaves,
My own face lay like a white pebble,
Waiting.

[ . . . ]

V

I followed a procession of singing girls
Who danced to the glitter of tambourines
Where the street turned at a lighted corner
I caught the purple dress of one of the dancers
But, as I grasped it, it tore,
And the purple dye ran from it,
Like blood
Upon the ground

[ . . . ]

VII

I had made a kite,
On it I had pasted golden stars
And white torches,
And the tail was spotted scarlet like a tiger-lily,
And very long.
I flew my kite,
And my soul was contented
Watching it flash against the concave of the sky.

My friends pointed at the clouds;
They begged me to take in my kite.
But I was happy
Seeing the mirror shock of it
Against the black clouds.
Then the lightning came
And struck the kite.
It puffed—blazed—fell.
But still I walked on,
In the drowning rain,
Slowly winding up the string.

*The Little Review,* June 1918


## A SPRIG OF ROSEMARY

I cannot see your face.
When I think of you,
It is your hands which I see.
Your hands
Sewing,
Holding a book,
Resting for a moment on the sill of a window.
My eyes keep always the sight of your hands,
But my heart holds the sound of your voice,
And the soft brightness which is your soul.

*Scribner's Magazine,* July 1918


## THE BROKEN FOUNTAIN

Oblong, its jutted ends rounding into circles,
The old sunken basin lies with its flat, marble lip
An inch below the terrace tiles.
Over the stagnant water
Slide reflections:

The blue-green of coned yews,
The purple and red of trailing fuchsias
Dripping out of marble urns,
Bright squares of sky
Ribbed by the wake of a swimming beetle.
Through the blue-bronze water
Wavers the pale uncertainty of a shadow.
An arm flashes through the reflections,
A breast is outlined with leaves.
Outstretched in the quiet water
The statue of a Goddess slumbers.
But when Autumn comes
The beech leaves cover her with a golden counter-pane.

*Tout le Monde,* February 1919


## THE WEATHERVANE POINTS SOUTH

I put your leaves aside,
One by one:
The stiff, broad outer leaves;
The smaller ones,
Pleasant to touch, veined with purple;
The glazed inner leaves.
One by one
I parted you from your leaves,
Until you stood up like a white flower
Swaying slightly in the evening wind.

White flower,
Flower of wax, of jade, of unstreaked agate;
Flower with surfaces of ice,
With shadows faintly crimson.
Where in all the garden is there such a flower?
The stars crowd through the lilac leaves
To look at you.
The low moon brightens you with silver.

The bud is more than the calyx.
There is nothing to equal a white bud,
Of no colour, and of all;
Burnished by moonlight,
Thrust upon by a softly-swinging wind.

*Vanity Fair,* June 1919


## THE ARTIST

Why do you subdue yourself in golds and purples?
Why do you dim yourself with folded silks?
Do you not see that I can buy brocades in any draper's shop,
And that I am choked in the twilight of all these colours.
How pale you would be, and startling,
How quiet;
But your curves would spring upward
Like a clear jet of flung water,
You would quiver like a shot-up spray of water,
You would waver, and relapse, and tremble.
And I too should tremble,
Watching.

Murex-dyes and tinsel—
And yet I think I could bear your beauty unshaded.

*Pictures of the Floating World,* September 1919


## VERNAL EQUINOX

The scent of hyacinths, like a pale mist, lies between me and
    my book;
And the South Wind, washing through the room,
Makes the candles quiver.
My nerves sting at a spatter of rain on the shutter,
And I am uneasy with the thrusting of green shoots

Outside, in the night.

Why are you not here to overpower me with your tense and
    urgent love?

*Pictures of the Floating World,* September 1919

## PENUMBRA

As I sit here in the quiet Summer night,
Suddenly, from the distant road, there comes
The grind and rush of an electric car.
And, from still farther off,
An engine puffs sharply,
Followed by the drawn-out shunting scrape of a freight train.
These are the sounds that men make
In the long business of living.
They will always make such sounds,
Years after I am dead and cannot hear them.

Sitting here in the Summer night,
I think of my death.
What will it be like for you then?
You will see my chair
With its bright chintz covering
Standing in the afternoon sunshine,
As now.
You will see my narrow table
At which I have written so many hours.
My dogs will push their noses into your hand,
And ask—ask—
Clinging to you with puzzled eyes.

The old house will still be here,
The old house which has known me since the beginning.
The walls which have watched me while I played:
Soldiers, marbles, paper-dolls,
Which have protected me and my books.

The front-door will gaze down among the old trees
Where, as a child, I hunted ghosts and Indians;
It will look out on the wide gravel sweep
Where I rolled my hoop,
And at the rhododendron bushes
Where I caught black-spotted butterflies.

The old house will guard you,
As I have done.
Its walls and rooms will hold you,
And I shall whisper my thoughts and fancies
As always,
From the pages of my books.

You will sit here, some quiet Summer night,
Listening to the puffing trains,
But you will not be lonely,
For these things are a part of me.
And my love will go on speaking to you
Through the chairs, and the tables, and the pictures,
As it does now through my voice,
And the quick, necessary touch of my hand.

*Pictures of the Floating World,* September 1919

## SEPTEMBER. 1918

This afternoon was the colour of water falling through
    sunlight;
The trees glittered with the tumbling of leaves;
The sidewalks shone like alleys of dropped maple leaves,
And the houses ran along them laughing out of square, open
    windows.
Under a tree in the park,
Two little boys, lying flat on their faces,
Were carefully gathering red berries
To put in a pasteboard box.

Some day there will be no war,
Then I shall take out this afternoon
And turn it in my fingers,
And remark the sweet taste of it upon my palate,
And note the crisp variety of its flights of leaves.
To-day I can only gather it
And put it into my lunch-box,
For I have time for nothing
But the endeavour to balance myself
Upon a broken world.

*Pictures of the Floating World*, September 1919


## GRANADILLA

I cut myself upon the thought of you
And yet I come back to it again and again,
A kind of fury makes me want to draw you out
From the dimness of the present
And set you sharply above me in a wheel of roses.
Then, going obviously to inhale their fragrance,
I touch the blade of you and cling upon it,
And only when the blood runs out across my fingers
Am I at all satisfied.

*Coterie,* Easter 1920


## CARREFOUR

O You,
Who came upon me once
Stretched under apple-trees just after bathing,
Why did you not strangle me before speaking
Rather than fill me with the wild white honey of your words
And then leave me to the mercy
Of the forest bees.

*Coterie,* Easter 1920

## LILACS

Lilacs,
False blue,
White,
Purple,
Color of lilac,
Your great puffs of flowers
Are everywhere in this my New England.
Among your heart-shaped leaves
Orange orioles hop like music-box birds and sing
Their little weak soft songs;
In the crooks of your branches
The bright eyes of song sparrows sitting on spotted eggs
Peer restlessly through the light and shadow
Of all Springs.
Lilacs in dooryards
Holding quiet conversations with an early moon;
Lilacs watching a deserted house
Settling sideways into the grass of an old road;
Lilacs, wind-beaten, staggering under a lopsided shock of
   bloom
Above a cellar dug into a hill.
You are everywhere.
You were everywhere.
You tapped the window when the preacher preached his
   sermon,
And ran along the road beside the boy going to school.
You stood by the pasture-bars to give the cows good milking,
You persuaded the housewife that her dishpan was of silver.
And her husband an image of pure gold.
You flaunted the fragrance of your blossoms
Through the wide doors of Custom Houses—
You, and sandal-wood, and tea,
Charging the noses of quill-driving clerks
When a ship was in from China.
You called to them: "Goose-quill men, goose-quill men,
May is a month for flitting."

Until they writhed on their high stools
And wrote poetry on their letter-sheets behind the
    propped-up ledgers.
Paradoxical New England clerks,
Writing inventories in ledgers, reading the "Song of Solomon"
    at night,
So many verses before bed-time,
Because it was the Bible.
The dead fed you
Amid the slant stones of graveyards.
Pale ghosts who planted you
Came in the nighttime
And let their thin hair blow through your clustered stems.
You are of the green sea,
And of the stone hills which reach a long distance.
You are of elm-shaded streets with little shops where they sell
    kites and marbles,
You are of great parks where every one walks and nobody is at
    home.
You cover the blind sides of greenhouses
And lean over the top to say a hurry-word through the glass
To your friends, the grapes, inside.

Lilacs,
False blue,
White,
Purple,
Color of lilac,
You have forgotten your Eastern origin,
The veiled women with eyes like panthers,
The swollen, aggressive turbans of jeweled pashas.
Now you are a very decent flower,
A reticent flower,
A curiously clear-cut, candid flower,
Standing beside clean doorways,
Friendly to a house-cat and a pair of spectacles,
Making poetry out of a bit of moonlight
And a hundred or two sharp blossoms.

Maine knows you,
Has for years and years;
New Hampshire knows you,
And Massachusetts
And Vermont.
Cape Cod starts you along the beaches to Rhode Island;
Connecticut takes you from a river to the sea.
You are brighter than apples,
Sweeter than tulips,
You are the great flood of our souls
Bursting above the leaf-shapes of our hearts,
You are the smell of all Summers,
The love of wives and children,
The recollection of gardens of little children,
You are State Houses and Charters
And the familiar treading of the foot to and fro on a road it
    knows.
May is lilac here in New England,
May is a thrush singing "Sun up!" on a tip-top ash tree,
May is white clouds behind pine-trees
Puffed out and marching upon a blue sky.
May is a green as no other,
May is much sun through small leaves,
May is soft earth,
And apple-blossoms,
And windows open to a South Wind.
May is full light wind of lilac
From Canada to Narragansett Bay.

Lilacs,
False blue,
White,
Purple,
Color of lilac.
Heart-leaves of lilac all over New England,
Roots of lilac under all the soil of New England,
Lilac in me because I am New England,
Because my roots are in it,

Because my leaves are of it,
Because my flowers are for it,
Because it is my country
And I speak to it of itself
And sing of it with my own voice
Since certainly it is mine.

*New York Evening Post*, September 18, 1920


## MEETING-HOUSE HILL

I must be mad, or very tired,
When the curve of a blue bay beyond a railroad track
Is shrill and sweet to me like the sudden springing of a tune,
And the sight of a white church above thin trees in a city
    square
Amazes my eyes as though it were the Parthenon.
Clear, reticent, superbly final,
With the pillars of its portico refined to a cautious elegance,
It dominates the weak trees,
And the shot of its spire
Is cool, and candid,
Rising into an unresisting sky.
Strange meeting-house
Pausing a moment upon a squalid hill-top.
I watch the spire sweeping the sky,
I am dizzy with the movement of the sky;
I might be watching a mast
With its royals set full
Straining before a two-reef breeze.
I might be sighting a tea-clipper,
Tacking into the blue bay,
Just back from Canton
With her hold full of green and blue porcelain
And a Chinese coolie leaning over the rail
Gazing at the white spire
With dull, sea-spent eyes.

*A Miscellany of American Poetry*, 1920

## FOOTING UP A TOTAL

I moved to the sound of gold, and brass, and heavily-clashed
    silver.
From the towers, the watchers see the flags of my coming:
Tall magenta flags
Stinging against a pattern of light blue.
Trumpets and tubas
Exult for me before the walls of cities,
And I pass the gates entangled in a dance of lifted
    tambourines.

But you—you come only as a harebell comes;
One day there is nothing, and the next your steepled bells
    are all,
The rest is back ground.
You are neither blue, nor violet, nor red,
But all these colours blent and faded to a charming weariness
    of tone.
I glare; you blossom.
Yes, alas! and when they have clanged me to my grave
Wrapped gaudily in pale blue and magenta;
When muted bugles and slacked drums
Have brayed a last quietus;
What then, my friend?

Why, someone coming from the funeral
Will see you standing, nodding underneath a hedge
(Picking or not is nothing).
Will that person remember bones and shouting do you think?
I fancy he will listen to the music
Shaken so lightly from your whispering bells
And think how very excellent a thing
A flower growing in a hedge most surely is.
And so, a fig for rotting carcasses.

Waiter, bring me a bottle of Lachrima Christi,
And mind you don't break the seal.

Your health, my highly unsuccessful confrère,
Rocking your seed-bells while I drift to ashes.
The future is the future, therefore—
Damn you!

*The Dial,* August 1921

## PARADOX

You are an amethyst to me,
Beating dark slabs of purple
Against quiet smoothnesses of heliotrope,
Sending the wine-colour of torches
Rattling up against an avalanche of pale windy leaves.

You enter my heart as twilight
Seeping softly among the ghosts of beeches
In a glade where the last light cleaves for an instant upon the
    swung lash of a water fall.
You oversweep me with the splendid flashing of your
    darkness,
And my flowers are tinted with the light of your thin grey
    moon.
An amethyst garden you are to me,
And in your sands I write my poems,
And plant my heart for you in deathless yew trees
That their leaves may shield you from the falling snow.

Open your purple palaces for my entertainment,
Welcome my feet upon your polished floors,
And keep in your brazier always
One red hot coal;
For I come at the times which suit me,
Morning or evening,
And I am cold when I come down the long alleys to you.

Clang the doors against the multitude who would follow me.
Is not this my chamber where I would sleep?

*Tempo: A Magazine of Poetry,* August 1921

## PURPLE GRACKLES

The grackles have come.
The smoothness of the morning is puckered with their
  incessant chatter
A sociable lot, these purple grackles,
Thousands of them strung across a long run of wind,
Thousands of them beating the air-ways with quick
  wing-jerks,
Spinning down the currents of the South.
Every year they come,
My garden is a place of solace and recreation evidently,
For they always pass a day with me.
With high good nature they tell me what I do not want to
  hear.
The grackles have come.
I am persuaded that grackles are birds;
But when they are settled in the trees,
I am inclined to declare them fruits
And the trees turned hybrid blackberry vines.
Blackness shining and bulging under leaves,
Does not that mean blackberries, I ask you?
Nonsense! The grackles have come.

Nonchalant highwaymen, pickpockets, second-story burglars,
Stealing away my little hope of Summer.
There is no stealthy robbing in this.
Who ever heard such a gabble of thieves' talk!
It seems they delight in unmasking my poor pretence.
Yes, now I see that the hydrangea blooms are rusty;
That the hearts of the golden glow are ripening to lustreless
  seeds;

That the garden is dahlia-coloured,
Flaming with its last over-hot hues;
That the sun is pale as a lemon too small to fill the
    picking-ring.
I did not see this yesterday,
But to-day the grackles have come.

They drop out of the trees
And strut in companies over the lawn,
Tired of flying, no doubt;
A grand parade to limber legs and give wings a rest.
I should build a great fish-pond for them,
Since it is evident that a bird-bath, meant to accommodate
    two goldfinches at most,
Is slight hospitality for these hordes.
Scarcely one can get in,
They all peck and scrabble so,
Crowding, pushing, chasing one another up the bank with
    spread wings.
"Are we ducks, you, owner of such inadequate comforts,
That you offer us lily-tanks where one must swim or drown,
Not stand and splash like a gentleman?"
I feel the reproach keenly, seeing them perch on the edges of
    the tanks, trying the depth with a chary foot,
And hardly able to get their wings under water in the
    bird-bath.
But there are resources I had not considered,
If I am bravely ruled out of count.
What is that thudding against the eaves just beyond my
    window?
What is that spray of water blowing past my face?
Two—three—grackles bathing in the gutter,
The gutter providentially choked with leaves.
I pray they think I put the leaves there on purpose;
I would be supposed thoughtful and welcoming
To all guests, even thieves.
But considering that they are going South and I am not,

I wish they would bathe more quietly,
It is unmannerly to flaunt one's good fortune.

They rate me of no consequence,
But they might reflect that it is my gutter.
I know their opinion of me,
Because one is drying himself on the window-sill
Not two feet from my hand.
His purple neck is sleek with water,
And the fellow preens his feathers for all the world as if I were
     a fountain statue.
If it were not for the window,
I am convinced he would light on my head.
Tyrian-feathered freebooter,
Appropriating my delightful gutter with so extravagant an
     ease,
You are as cool a pirate as ever scuttled a ship,
And are you not scuttling my Summer with every peck of
     your sharp bill?

But there is a cloud over the beech-tree,
A quenching cloud for lemon-livered suns.
The grackles are all swinging in the tree-tops,
And the wind is coming up, mind you.
That boom and reach is no Summer gale,
I know that wind,
It blows the Equinox over seeds and scatters them,
It rips petals from petals, and tears off half-turned leaves.
There is rain on the back of that wind.
Now I would keep the grackles,
I would plead with them not to leave me.
I grant their coming, but I would not have them go.
It is a milestone, this passing of grackles.
A day of them, and it is a year gone by.
There is magic in this and terror,
But I only stare stupidly out of the window.
The grackles have come.

Come! Yes, they surely came.
But they have gone.
A moment ago the oak was full of them,
They are not there now.
Not a speck of a black wing,
Not an eye-peep of a purple head.
The grackles have gone,
And I watch an Autumn storm
Stripping the garden,
Shouting black rain challenges
To an old, limp Summer
Laid down to die in the flower-beds.

*The Bookman,* July 1922


## IN EXCELSIS

You—you—
Your shadow is sunlight on a plate of silver;
Your footsteps, the seeding-place of lilies;
Your hands moving, a chime of bells across a windless air.

The movement of your hands is the long, golden running of
    light from a rising sun;
It is the hopping of birds upon a garden-path.

As the perfume of jonquils, you come forth in the morning.
Young horses are not more sudden than your thoughts,
Your words are bees about a pear-tree;
Your fancies are the gold-and-black-striped wasps buzzing
    among red apples.
I drink your lips;
I eat the whiteness of your hands and feet.
My mouth is open;
As a new jar I am empty and open.
Like white water are you who fill the cup of my mouth;
Like a brook of water thronged with lilies.

You are frozen as the clouds;
You are far and sweet as the high clouds.
I dare reach to you;
I dare touch the rim of your brightness.
I leap beyond the winds,
I cry and shout,
For my throat is keen as a sword
Sharpened on a hone of ivory.
My throat sings the joy of my eyes,
The rushing gladness of my love.

How has the rainbow fallen upon my heart?
How have I snared the seas to lie in my fingers
And caught the sky to be a cover for my head?
How have you come to dwell with me,
Compassing me with the four circles of your mystic lightness,
So that I say "Glory! Glory!" and bow before you
As to a shrine?

Do I tease myself that morning is morning and a day after?
Do I think the air a condescension,
The earth a politeness,
Heaven a boon deserving thanks?
So you,—air,—earth,—heaven—
I do not thank you;
I take you,
I live.
And those things which I say in consequence
Are rubies mortised in a gate of stone.

*The Century,* September 1922

## ON READING A LINE UNDERSCORED BY KEATS
### IN A COPY OF "PALMERIN OF ENGLAND"

You marked it with light pencil upon a printed page,
And, as though your finger pointed along a sunny path for my
    eyes' better direction,

I see "a knight mounted on a mulberry courser and attired in
   green armour."
I think the sky is faintly blue, but with a spring shining
   about it,
And the new grass scarcely fetlock high in the meads.
He rides, I believe, alongside an overflown river,
By a path soft and easy to his charger's feet.
My vision confuses you with the green-armoured knight:
So dight and caparisoned might you be in a land of faery.
Thus, with denoting finger, you make of yourself an
   escutcheon to guide me to that in you which is its essence.
But for the rest,
The part which most persists and is remembered,
I only know I compass it in loving and neither have, nor need,
   a symbol.

*The Literary Review, New York Evening Post,* October 7, 1922

## DISSONANCE

From my window I can see the moonlight stroking the
   smooth surface of the river.
The trees are silent, there is no wind.
Admirable pre-Raphaelite landscape,
Lightly touched with ebony and silver.
I alone am out of keeping:
An angry red gash
Proclaiming the restlessness
Of an incongruous century.

*Rhythmus: A Magazine of the New Poetry,* January 1923

## HERALDIC

I have often a vision of your face,
Seen through the crossing branches of young trees.
Your face, as a white, flowing water,

At a little distance, beyond the reeds of a shallow shore.
Ironical, my lady, that Spring, the barb and whetstone of my
 love,
Should net you from me in leaves and whisperings!
Yet I would not lose even this,
Although the sight and leashing tease me to madness.

         *Prairie,* January and February 1923


## ATTITUDE UNDER AN ELM TREE

Seeing that you pass your life playing upon the virginals
In an upper chamber with only a slit of a window in it,
I wonder why I,
Roaming the hills on a charger red as maple-leaves,
Should find the thought of you attractive.
You were veiled at the jousting, you remember,
Which enables me to imagine you without let or hindrance
 from the rigidness of fact;
A condition not unproductive of charm if viewed
 philosophically.
Besides, your window gives upon a walled garden,
Which I can by no means enter without dismounting from
 my maple-red charger,
And this I will not do,
Particularly as the garden belongs indubitably to your
 ancestors.
But I thank you for the spray of myrtle I have wound about
 my sleeve.
As it over-topped the wall,
My plucking it was without malice.

    *The Literary Review, New York Evening Post,* August 18, 1923


## SULTRY

To those who can see them, there are eyes:
Leopard eyes of marigolds crouching above red earth,
Bulging eyes of fruits and rubies in the heavily-hanging trees,

Broken eyes of queasy cupids staring from the gloom of
    myrtles.
I came here for solitude
And I am plucked at by a host of eyes.

A peacock spreads his tail on the balustrade
And every eye is a mood of green malice,
A challenge and a fear.
A hornet flashes above geraniums,
Spying upon me in a trick of cunning.
And Hermes,
Hermes the implacable,
Points at me with a fractured arm.

Vengeful god of smooth, imperishable loveliness,
You are more savage than the goat-legged Pan,
Than the crocodile of carven yew-wood.
Fisherman of men's eyes,
You catch them on a three-pronged spear:
Your youth, your manhood,
The reticence of your everlasting revelation.
I too am become a cunning eye
Seeking you past your time-gnawed surface,
Seeking you back to hyacinths upon a dropping hill,
Where legend drowses in a glaze of sea.

Yours are the eyes of a bull and a panther,
For all that they are chiseled out and the sockets empty.
You—perfectly imperfect,
Clothed in a garden,
In innumerable gardens,
Borrowing the eyes of fruits and flowers—
And mine also, cold, impossible god,
So that I stare back at myself
And see myself with loathing.

A quince-tree flings a crooked shadow—
My shadow, tortured out of semblance,

Bewildered in quince boughs.
His shadow is clear as a scissored silhouette.
Heat twinkles and the eyes glare.
And I, of the mingled shadow,
I glare
And see nothing.

*The Dial,* December 1923


## THE ON-LOOKER

Suppose I plant you
Like wide-eyed Helen
On the battlements
Of weary Troy,
Clutching the parapet with desperate hands.
She, too, gazes at a battle-field
Where bright vermilion plumes and metal whiteness
Shock and sparkle and go down with groans.
Her glances strike the rocking battle,
Again—again—
Recoiling from it
Like baffled spear-heads fallen from a brazen shield.
The ancients at her elbow counsel patience and contingencies;
Such to a woman stretched upon a bed of battle,
Who bargained for this only in the whispering arras
Enclosed about a midnight of enchantment.

*Saturday Review of Literature,* February 1925


## POETIC JUSTICE

Double-flowering trees bear no fruit, they say,
And I have many blossoms,
With petals shrewdly whirled about an empty center,
White as paper, falling at a whiff of wind.
But when they are gone

There are only green leaves to catch at the sunlight,
Green monotonous leaves
Which hide nothing.

*The Bookman,* July 1925


## MID-ADVENTURE

Mist, vapour,
A little whiff of wind,
Noticed as nothing and as soon forgotten,
Such was my purpose.
It would have held, too,
No doubt of that,
And you and I no other than we were.
You would not have it so.
Your call cloaked me in the seeming of reality,
I entered, bidden, to your consciousness.
And here I stand,
Waiting, for so you will for me,
Waiting.
For what?
Would you have me like a caryatid,
Holding above your head some sheltering sky
Of softened, tempered sunlight?
Would you keep me as a gathered curio
To say: "See, this I found, and kept for luck"?
Or do you guess at possibilities,
A warmth to draw from me when nights grow cold
And gates whine bitterly in window cracks?
For myself,
I have lost recollection how I came.
Returning shows a dim, uneasy way
My feet refuse to follow.
Yet suppose,
Suppose the very custom of my long

Vacant delaying just inside the door
Blurs me to an impassive bibelot,
A bit of furniture which, neither used
Nor looked at, is most likely to be left
Totally unregarded and ignored—
My summons nothing,
A caprice outworn—
Standing forsaken in an empty room.
How the wind howls!
The fire is a red recumbent ash.
The future, strange chameleon to the drift of time,
Turns round on me a grinning pasteboard face
Dropped from a masker at a carnival.
Hola! then. I'll be harlequin and dance
In checkers of blood-red and black hearse plumes,
Capering, dead drunk, upon a coffin lid.

*Ballads for Sale,* September 1927

## ANECDOTE

First Soliloquy
Her breasts were small, upright, virginal;
Even through her clothes I could feel the nipples pointing
    upward when I touched her inadvertently.
The chastity of her garments was pronounced,
But no disposal of material could keep the shape of her breasts
    unseen.

And you would walk as a Spring wind,
You would order your demeanour as though there were still
    frost in the air,
You would keep me to my distance by the cool agreeableness
    of your speech.
You are foolish, Madam, or deceived.
Is it possible you underrate my sensibility

And do not realize that I hold your breasts
In the hollow of my hand?

## SECOND SOLILOQUY

His voice was a dagger tipped with honey,
His touch a scimitar dripping myrrh and gall.
He parted me from myself
And I stood alone in sunshine and trembled.
I caught my garments about me,
But they withered one by one as leaves wither, and fell.
I was alone in the wide sunlight;
His eyes were winds which would not leave me.
I would have sought a tree,
But the place where I was was bare and light.
Merciless light he shed upon me,
And I stretched my arms in shame and rejoicing.
Why do you stand there watching me?
Are you blind to what is really happening
That you talk so lightly of trifles?
Stop talking, you suffocate me.
Does any one notice?
Why do you strip me before all these people -
You, who care nothing for my nakedness?
Unbearable the anguish of my body,
The ache of my breasts,
The strain of covering myself is choking me.
Why do you do nothing but talk?
Have you no hands, no heart,
Or are you so cynical that you expose me for a whim?
Oh, I am well-trained, be sure of that,
But can you not see through my pretense?
It is agony to hold myself away from you,
Yet you are as impassive as a stone Hermes before whom
    Venus herself would need no cloak.
Now that you are gone, what have you left me?
No privacy at all, I think.

You have stolen my secrecy, and flung it back as something
    not worth taking.
I have only the harsh memory of your eyes,
Your dull, stone eyes which haunt me in the dark.

*Ballads for Sale,* September 1927


## STILL LIFE
### MOONLIGHT STRIKING UPON A CHESS-BOARD

I am so aching to write
That I could make a song out of a chess-board
And rhyme the intrigues of knights and bishops
And the hollow fate of a checkmated king.
I might have been a queen, but I lack the proper century;
I might have been a poet, but where is the adventure to
    explode me into flame.
Cousin Moon, our kinship is curiously demonstrated,
For I, too, am a bright, cold corpse
Perpetually circling above a living world.

*Ballads for Sale,* September 1927

# POLYPHONIC
# PROSE

The form is so called because it makes use of all the "voices" of
poetry, viz.: metre, *vers libre,* assonance, alliteration, rhyme, and
return. It employs every form of rhythm, even prose rhythm at
times, but usually holds no particular one for long.

—AMY LOWELL, "John Gould Fletcher," in
*Tendencies in Modern American Poetry*

# SPRING DAY

## BATH

The day is fresh-washed and fair, and there is a smell of tulips and narcissus in the air.

The sunshine pours in at the bath-room window and bores through the water in the bath-tub in lathes and planes of greenish-white. It cleaves the water into flaws like a jewel, and cracks it to bright light.

Little spots of sunshine lie on the surface of the water and dance, dance, and their reflections wobble deliciously over the ceiling; a stir of my finger sets them whirring, reeling. I move a foot and the planes of light in the water jar. I lie back and laugh, and let the green-white water, the sun-flawed beryl water, flow over me. The day is almost too bright to bear, the green water covers me from the too bright day. I will lie here awhile and play with the water and the sun spots. The sky is blue and high. A crow flaps by the window, and there is a whiff of tulips and narcissus in the air.

## BREAKFAST TABLE

In the fresh-washed sunlight, the breakfast table is decked and white. It offers itself in flat surrender, tendering tastes, and smells, and colours, and metals, and grains, and the white cloth falls over its side, draped and wide. Wheels of white glitter in the silver coffee-pot, hot and spinning like Catherine-wheels, they whirl, and twirl—and my eyes begin to smart, the little white, dazzling wheels prick them like darts. Placid and peaceful the rolls of bread spread themselves in the sun to bask. A stack of butter-pats, pyramidal, shout orange through the white, scream, flutter, call: "Yellow! Yellow! Yellow!" Coffee steam rises in a stream, clouds the silver tea-service with mist, and twists up into the sunlight, revolved, involuted, suspiring higher and higher, fluting in a thin spiral up the high blue sky. A crow flies by and croaks at the coffee steam. The day is new and fair with good smells in the air.

## WALK

Over the street the white clouds meet, and sheer away without touching.

On the sidewalks, boys are playing marbles. Glass marbles, with amber and blue hearts, roll together and part with a sweet clashing noise. The boys strike them with black and red striped agates. The glass marbles spit crimson when they are hit, and slip into the gutters under rushing brown water. I smell tulips and narcissus in the air, but there are not flowers anywhere, only white dust whipping up the street, and a girl with a gay spring hat and blowing skirts. The dust and the wind flirt at her ankles and her neat, high-heeled patent leather shoes. Tap, tap, the little heels pat the pavement, and the wind rustles among the flowers on her hat.

A water-cart crawls slowly on the other side of the way. It is green and gay with new paint, and rumbles contentedly, sprinkling clear water over the white dust. Clear zigzagging water, which smells of tulips and narcissus.

The thickening branches make a pink "grisaille" against the blue sky.

Whoop! The clouds go dashing at each other and sheer away just in time. Whoop! And a man's hat careers down the street in front of the white dust, leaps into the branches of a tree, veers away and trundles ahead of the wind, jarring the sunlight into spokes of rose-colour and green.

A motor-car cuts a swathe through the bright air, sharp-beaked, irresistible, shouting to the wind to make way. A glare of dust and sunshine tosses together behind it, and settles down. The sky is quiet and high, and the morning is fair with fresh-washed air.

## MIDDAY AND AFTERNOON

Swirl of crowded streets. Shock and recoil of traffic. The stock-still brick façade of an old church, against which the waves of people lurch and withdraw. Flare of sunshine down side-streets. Eddies of light in the windows of chemists' shops, with their blue, gold, purple jars, darting colours far into the crowd. Loud bangs and tremors, murmurings out of high windows, whirring of machine-belts, blurring of horses and motors. A quick spin and shudder of brakes on an electric car, and the jar of a church-bell knocking against the metal blue of the sky. I am a piece of the town, a bit of the sky. I am a piece of the town, a bit of blown dust, thrust along with the crowd. Proud to feel the pavement under me, reeling with feet. Feet tripping, skipping, lagging, dragging, plodding doggedly, or springing up and advancing on firm elastic insteps. A boy is selling papers, I smell them clean and new from the press. They are fresh like the air, and pungent as tulips and narcissus.

The blue sky pales to lemon, and great tongues of gold blind the shop-windows, putting out their contents in a flood of flame.

## NIGHT AND SLEEP

The day takes her ease in slippered yellow. Electric signs gleam out along the shop fronts, following each other. They grow, and grow, and blow into patterns of fire-flowers as the sky fades. Trades scream in spots of light at the unruffled night. Twinkle, jab, snap, that means a new play; and over the way: plop, drop, quiver, is the sidelong sliver of a watchmaker's sign with its length on another street. A gigantic mug of beer effervesces to the atmosphere over a tall building, but the sky is high and has her own stars, why should she heed ours?

I leave the city with speed. Wheels whirl to take me back to my trees and my quietness. The breeze which blows with me is fresh-washed and clean, it has come but recently from the high sky. There are no flowers in bloom yet, but the earth of my garden smells of tulips and narcissus.

My room is tranquil and friendly. Out of the window I can see the distant city, a band of twinkling gems, little flower-heads with no stems. I cannot see the beer glass, nor the letters of the restaurants and shops I passed, now the signs blur and all together make the city, glowing on a night of fine weather, like a garden stirring and blowing for the Spring.

The night is fresh-washed and fair and there is a whiff of flowers in the air.

Wrap me close, sheets of lavender. Pour your blue and purple dreams into my ears. The breeze whispers at the shutters and mutters queer tales of old days, and cobbled streets, and youths leaping their horses down marble stairways. Pale blue lavender, you are the colour of the sky when it is fresh-washed and fair . . . I smell the stars . . . they are like tulips and narcissus . . . I smell them in the air.

*The Egoist,* May 1915

# FROM MALMAISON

## I

How the slates of the roof sparkle in the sun, over there, over there, beyond the high wall! How quietly the Seine runs in loops and windings, over there, over there, sliding through the green countryside! Like ships of the line, stately with canvas, the tall clouds pass along the sky, over the glittering roof, over the trees, over the looped and curving river. A breeze quivers through the linden-trees. Roses bloom at Malmaison. Roses! Roses! But the road is dusty. Already the Citoyenne Beauharnais wearies of her walk. Her skin is chalked and powdered with dust, she smells dust, and behind the wall are roses! Roses with smooth open petals, poised above rippling leaves . . . Roses . . . They have told her so. The Citoyenne Beauharnais shrugs her shoulders and makes a little face. She must mend her pace if she would be back in time for dinner. Roses indeed! The guillotine more likely.

The tiered clouds float over Malmaison, and the slate roof sparkles in the sun.

## II

Gallop! Gallop! The General brooks no delay. Make way, good people, and scatter out of his path, you, and your hens, and your dogs, and your children. The General is returned from Egypt, and is come in a *calèche* and four to visit his new property. Throw open the gates, you, Porter of Malmaison. Pull off your cap, my man, this is your master, the husband of Madame. Faster! Faster! A jerk and a jingle and they are arrived, he and she. Madame has red eyes.

Fie! It is for joy at her husband's return. Learn your place, Porter.
A gentleman here for two months? Fie! Fie, then! Since when have
you taken to gossiping. Madame may have a brother, I suppose.
That—all green, and red, and glitter, with flesh as dark as ebony—
that is a slave; a bloodthirsty, stabbing, slashing heathen, come
from the hot countries to cure your tongue of idle whispering.

A fine afternoon it is, with tall bright clouds sailing over the
trees.

"Bonaparte, mon ami, the trees are golden like my star, the star
I pinned to your destiny when I married you. The gypsy, you re-
member her prophecy! My dear friend, not here, the servants are
watching; send them away, and that flashing splendour, Roustan.
Superb—Imperial, but . . . My dear, your arm is trembling; I faint
to feel it touching me! No, no, Bonaparte, not that—spare me
that—did we not bury that last night! You hurt me, my friend, you
are so hot and strong. Not long, Dear, no, thank God, not long."
      The looped river runs saffron, for the sun is setting. It is getting
dark. Dark. Darker. In the moonlight, the slate roof shines palely
milkily white.
      The roses have faded at Malmaison, nipped by the frost. What
need for roses? Smooth, open petals—her arms. Fragrant, out-
curved petals—her breasts. He rises like a sun above her, stoop-
ing to touch the petals, press them wider. Eagles. Bees. What are
they to open roses! A little shivering breeze runs through the lin-
den-trees, and the tiered clouds blow across the sky like ships of
the line, stately with canvas.
[ . . . ]

V

The roses bloom at Malmaison. And not only roses. Tulips,
myrtles, geraniums, camelias, rhododendrons, dahlias, double hy-
acinths. All the year through, under glass, under the sky, flow-
ers bud, expand, die, and give way to others, always others. From
distant countries they have been brought, and taught to live in the

cool temperateness of France. There is the *Bonapartea* from Peru; the *Napoleone Imperiale;* the *Josephinia Imperatrix,* a pearl-white flower, purple-shadowed, the calix pricked out with crimson points. Malmaison wears its flowers as a lady wears her gems, flauntingly, assertively. Malmaison decks herself to hide the hollow within.

The glass-houses grow and grow, and every year fling up hotter reflections to the sailing sun.

The cost runs into millions, but a woman must have something to console herself for a broken heart. One can play backgammon and patience, and then patience and backgammon, and stake gold napoleons on each game won. Sport truly! It is an unruly spirit which could ask better. With her jewels, her laces, her shawls; her two hundred and twenty dresses, her fichus, her veils; her pictures, her busts, her birds. It is absurd that she cannot be happy. The Emperor smarts under the thought of her ingratitude. What could he do more? And yet she spends, spends as never before. It is ridiculous. Can she not enjoy life at a smaller figure? Was ever monarch plagued with so extravagant an ex-wife. She owes her chocolate-merchant, her candle-merchant, her sweetmeat purveyor; her grocer, her butcher, her poulterer; her architect, and the shopkeeper who sells her rouge; her perfumer, her dressmaker, her merchant of shoes. She owes for fans, plants, engravings, and chairs. She owes masons and carpenters, vintners, *lingères.* The lady's affairs are in sad confusion.

And why? Why?
Can a river flow when the spring is dry?

Night. The Empress sits alone, and the clock ticks, one after one. The clock nicks off the edges of her life. She is chipped like an old bit of china; she is frayed like a garment of last year's wearing. She is soft, crinkled, like a fading rose. And each minute flows by brushing against her, shearing off another and another petal. The Empress crushes her breasts with her hands and weeps. And the tall clouds sail over Malmaison like a procession of stately ships bound for the moon.

Scarlet, clear-blue, purple epauletted with gold. It is a parade of soldiers sweeping up the avenue. Eight horses, eight Imperial harnesses, four caparisoned postilions, a carriage with the Emperor's arms on the panels. Ho, Porter, pop out your eyes, and no wonder. Where else under the Heavens could you see such splendour!

They sit on a stone seat. The little man in the green coat of a Colonel of Chasseurs, and the lady, beautiful as a satin seed-pod, and as pale. The house has memories. The satin seed-pod holds his germs of Empire. We will stay here, under the blue sky and the turreted white clouds. She draws him; he feels her faded loveliness urge him to replenish it. Her soft transparent texture woos his nervous fingering. He speaks to her of debts, of resignation; of her children, and his; he promises that she shall see the King of Rome; he says some harsh things and some pleasant. But she is there, close to him, rose toned to amber, white shot with violet, pungent to his nostrils as embalmed roseleaves in a twilit room.

Suddenly the Emperor calls his carriage and rolls away across the looping Seine.

[ . . . ]


## VII


Over the slate roof tall clouds, like ships of the line, pass along the sky. The glass-houses glitter splotchily, for many of their lights are broken. Roses bloom, fiery cinders quenching under damp weeds. Wreckage and misery, and a trailing of petty deeds smearing over old recollections.

The musty rooms are empty and their shutters are closed, only in the gallery there is a stuffed black swan, covered with dust. When you touch it, the feathers come off and float softly to the ground. Through a chink in the shutters, one can see the stately clouds crossing the sky toward the Roman arches of the Marly Aqueduct.

*The Little Review,* June–July 1916

# FROM SEA-BLUE AND BLOOD-RED

(POLYPHONIC PROSE)

## THE MEDITERRANEAN

Blue as the tip of a salvia blossom, the inverted cup of the sky arches over the sea. Up to meet it, in a flat band of glaring colour, rises the water. The sky is unspecked by clouds, but the sea is flecked with pink and white light shadows, and silver scintillations snip-snap over the tops of the waves.

Something moves along the horizon. A puff of wind blowing up the edges of the silver-blue sky? Clouds! Clouds! Great thunderheads marching along the skyline! No, by Jove! The sun shining on sails! Vessels, hull down, with only their tiers of canvas showing. Beautiful ballooning thunderheads dipping one after another below the blue band of the sea.

## NAPLES

Red tiles, yellow stucco, layer on layer of windows, roofs, and balconies, Naples pushes up the hill away from the curving bay. A red, half-closed eye, Vesuvius watches and waits. All Naples prates of this and that, and runs about its little business, shouting, bawling, incessantly calling its wares. Fish frying, macaroni drying, seven feet piles of red and white broccoli, grapes heaped high with rosemary, sliced pomegranates dripping seeds, plucked and bleeding chickens, figs on spits, lemons in baskets, melons cut and quartered nicely, "*Ah, che bella cosa!*" They even sell water, clear crystal water for a *paul* or two. And everything done to a hulla-baloo. They jabber over cheese, they chatter over wine, they gab-ble at the corners in the bright sunshine. And piercing through the noise is the beggar-whine, always, like an undertone, the beggar-whine; and always the crimson, watching eye of Vesuvius.

Have you seen her—the Ambassadress? Ah, *Bellissima Creatura! Una Donna Rara!* She is fairer than the Blessed Virgin; and good! Never was such a soul in such a body! The rôle of her benefactions would stretch from here to Posillipo. And she loves the people, loves to go among them and speak to this one and that, and her apple-blossom face under the big blue hat works miracles like the Holy Images in the Churches.

In her great house with the red marble stairway, Lady Hamilton holds brilliant sway. From her boudoir windows she can see the bay, and on the left, hanging there, a flame in a cresset, the blood-red glare of Vesuvius staring at the clear blue air.

Blood-red on a night of stars, red like a wound, with lava scars. In the round wall-mirrors of her boudoir, is the blackness of the bay, the whiteness of a star, and the bleeding redness of the moun-tain's core. Nothing more. All night long, in the mirrors, nothing more. Black water, red stain, and above, a star with its silver rain.

Over the people, over the king, trip the little Ambassadorial feet; fleet and light as a pigeon's wing, they brush over the artists, the friars, the *abbés,* the Court. They bear her higher and higher at each step. Up and over the hearts of Naples goes the beautiful Lady Hamilton till she reaches even to the Queen; then rests in a sheen-ing, shimmering altitude, between earth and sky, high and floating as the red crater of Vesuvius. Buoyed up and sustained in a blood-red destiny, all on fire for the world to see.

Proud Lady Hamilton! Superb Lady Hamilton! Quivering, blood-swept, vivid Lady Hamilton! Your vigor is enough to awake the dead, as you tread the newly uncovered courtyards of Pompeii. There is a murmur all over the opera house when you enter your box. And your frocks! Jesu! What frocks! "India painting on wyte sattin!" And a new camlet shawl, all sea-blue and blood-red, in an intricate pattern, given by Sir William to help you do your mar-velous "Attitudes." Incomparable actress! No theatre built is big enough to compass you. It takes a world; and centuries shall elbow each other aside to watch you act your part. Art, Emma, or heart?

The blood-red cone of Vesuvius glows in the night.

She sings "*Luce Bella*," and Naples cries "*Brava! Ancora!*" and claps its hands. She dances the tarantella, and poses before a screen with the red-blue shawl. It is the frescoes of Pompeii unfrozen; it is the fine-cut profiles of Sicilian coins; it is Apollo Belvedere him-self—Goethe has said it. She wears a Turkish dress, and her face is sweet and lively as rippled water.

The lava-streams of Vesuvius descend as far as Portici. She climbs the peak of fire at midnight—five miles of flame. A blood-red mountain, seeping tears of blood. She skips over glowing ashes and laughs at the pale, faded moon, wan in the light of the red-hot lava. What a night! Spires and sparks of livid flame shooting into the black sky. Blood-red smears of fire; blood-red gashes, flash-ing her out against the smoldering mountain. A tossing fountain of blood-red jets, it sets her hair flicking into the air like licking flamelets of a burning aureole. Blood-red is everywhere. She wears it as a halo and diadem. Emma, Emma Hamilton, Ambassadress of Great Britain to the Kingdom of the Two Sicilies.

## ABOUKIR BAY, EGYPT

North-north-west, and a whole-sail breeze, ruffling up the lark-spur-blue sea, breaking the tops of the waves into egg-white foam, shoving ripple after ripple of pale jade-green over the shoals of Aboukir Bay. Away to the East rolls in the sluggish water of old Nile. West and South—hot, yellow land. Ships at anchor. Thirteen ships flying the *tricolore,* and riding at ease in a patch of blue wa-ter inside a jade-green hem. What of them? Ah, fine ships! The *Orient,* one hundred and twenty guns, *Franklin, Tonnant,* each with eighty. Weighty metal to float on a patch of blue with a green hem.

They ride stem to stern, in a long line, pointing the way to Abou-kir Bay.

To the North are thunderheads, ballooning silver white thunderheads rising up out of the horizon. The thunderheads draw steadily up into the blue-blossomed sky. A topgallant breeze pushes them rapidly over the white-specked water. One, Two, Six, Ten, Thirteen separate tiered clouds, and the wind sings loud in their shrouds and spars. The royals are furled, but the topgallant-sails and topsails are full and straining. Thirteen white thunderheads bearing down on Aboukir Bay.

[ . . . ]

Round to starboard swing the white thunderheads, the water of their bows washing over the green jade hem. An orange sunset steams in the shrouds, and gluts upon the muzzles of the cannon in the open ports. The hammocks are down; the guns run out and primed; beside each is a pile of canister and grape; gunners are blowing on their matches; snatches of fife music drift down to the lower decks. In the cockpits, the surgeons are feeling the edges of knives and saws; men think of their wives and swear softly, spitting on their hands.

"Let go that anchor! By God, she hangs!"

Past the *Guerrier* slides the *Goliath*, but the anchor drops and stops her on the inner quarter of the *Conquérant*. The *Zealous* brings up on the bow of the *Guerrier*, the *Orion*, *Theseus*, *Audacious*, are all come to, inside the French ships.

The *Vanguard*, Admiral's pennant flying, is lying outside the *Spartiate*, distant only a pistol shot.

In a pattern like a country dance, each balanced justly by its neighbor, lightly, with no apparent labour, the ships slip into place, and lace a design of white sails and yellow yards on the purple, flowing water. Almighty Providence, what a day! Twenty-three ships in one small bay, and away to the eastward, the water of old Nile rolling sluggishly between its sand-bars.

Seven hundred and forty guns open fire on the French fleet. The sun sinks into the purple-red water, its low, straight light playing gold on the slaughter. Yellow fire, shot with red, in wheat sheafs from the guns; and a racket and ripping which jerks the nerves, then stuns, until another broadside crashes the ears alive again. The men shine with soot and sweat, and slip in the blood which wets the deck.

[ . . . ]

The day is fair. In the clear Egyptian air, the water of Aboukir Bay is as blue as the bottom flowers of a larkspur spray. The shoals are green with a white metal sheen, and between its sand-bars the Nile can be seen, slowly rolling out to sea.

[ . . . ]

## NAPLES

[ . . . ]

In the evenings, by the light of two wax candles, the Admiral writes kind acknowledgements to the tributes of half a world. Moslem and Christian sweetly united to stamp out liberty. It is an inspiring sight to see. Rule Britannia indeed, with Slavs and Turks boosting up her footstool. The Sultan has sent a Special Envoy bearing gifts: the Chelenck—"Plume of Triumph," all in diamonds, and a pelisse of sables, just as bonds of his eternal gratitude. "*Viva il Turco!*" says Lady Hamilton. The Mother of His Sultanic Majesty begs that the Admiral's pocket may be the repository of a diamond-studded box to hold his snuff. The Russian Tzar, a bit self-centred as most monarchs are, sends him his portrait, diamond-framed of course. The King of Sardinia glosses over his fewer gems by the richness of his compliments. The East India Company, secure of its trade, has paid him ten thousand pounds. The Turkish Company has given him plate. A grateful country augments his state by creating him the smallest kind of peer, with a couple of tuppences a year, and veneering it over by a grant of arms. Arms for an arm, but what for an eye! Does the Admiral smile as he writes his reply? Writes with his left hand that he is aware of the high honor it will be to bear this shield: "A chief undulated argent, from which a palm-tree issuant, between a disabled ship on the dexter, and a ruinous battery on the sinister, all proper." "Very proper, indeed," nods Sir William, but Lady Hamilton prods the colored paper shield a trifle scornfully. "If I was King of England, I would make you Duke Nelson, Marquis Nile, Earl Aboukir, Viscount Pyramid, Baron Crocodile and, Prince Victory." "My dear Emma, what a child you are," says Sir William, but the Admiral looks out of the window at the blood-red mountain and says nothing at all.

[ . . . ]

They are afloat, off the trembling, quivering soil of Naples, and their way is lit by a blood-red glimmer from the tossing fires of Vesuvius.

[ . . . ]

## AT SEA, OFF CAPE TRAFALGAR

Blue as the tip of a deep blue salvia blossom, the inverted cup of the sky arches over the sea. Up to meet it, in a concave curve of bright colour, rises the water, flat, unrippled, for the wind scarcely stirs. How comes the sky so full of clouds on the horizon, with none over head? Clouds! Great clouds of canvas! Mighty ballooning clouds, bearing thunder and crinkled lightning in their folds. They roll up out of the horizon, tiered, stately. Sixty-four great thunder-clouds, more perhaps, throwing their shadows over ten miles of sea.

Boats dash back and forth. Their ordered oars sparkling like silver as they lift and fall. Frigate captains receiving instructions, coming aboard the flagship, departing from it. Blue and white, with a silver flashing of boats.

Thirty-three clouds headed South, twenty-three others converging upon them! They move over the water as silently as the drifting air. Lines to lines, drawing nearer on the faint impulse of the breeze.

Blue coated, flashing with stars, the Admiral walks, up and down the poop. Stars on his breast, in his eyes the white glare of the sea. The enemy wears, looping end to end, and waits, poised in a half-circle like a pale new moon upon the water. The British ships point straight to the hollow between the horns, and even their stu'nsails are set. Arrows flung at a crescent over smooth blue water.

[ . . . ]

Boom! A shot passes through the main topgallantsail of the *Victory*. The ship is under fire. Her guns cannot bear while she is head on. Straight at the floating half-moon of ships goes the *Victory*, leading her line, muffled in the choking smoke of the *Bucentaure's* guns. The sun is dimmed, but through the smoke-cloud prick diamond sparkles from the Admiral's stars as he walks up and down the quarter-deck. Red glare of guns in the Admiral's eyes. Red stripe of marines drawn up on the poop. Eight are carried off by a single shot, and the red stripe liquefies, and seeps, lapping, down the gangway. Every stu'nsail boom is shot away. The blue of the sea has vanished; there is only the red of cannon, and the white twinkling sparks of the Admiral's stars.

The bows of the *Victory* cross the wake of the *Bucentaure*, and one after another, as they bear, the double-shotted guns tear through the woodwork of the French ship. The *Victory* slips past like a shooting shuttle, and runs on board the *Redoubtable*, seventy-four, and their spars lock, with a shock which almost stops their headway.

It is a glorious Autumn day outside the puff-ball of smoke. A still, blue sea, unruffled, banded to silver by a clear sun.

Guns of the *Victory*, guns of the *Redoubtable*, exploding incessantly, making one long draw of sound. Rattling upon it, rain on a tin roof, the pop-pop of muskets from the mizzen-top of the *Redoubtable*. There are sharpshooters in the mizzen-top, aiming at the fog below. Suddenly, through it, spears the gleam of diamonds; it is the Admiral's stars, reflecting the flashes of the guns.

Red blood in a flood before his eyes. Red from horizon to zenith, crushing down like beaten metal. The Admiral falls to his knees, to his side, and lies there, and the crimson glare closes over him, a cupped inexorable end. "They have done for me at last, Hardy. My back-bone is shot through."

The blue thread is snapped and the bolt falls from the loom. Weave, shuttle of the red thread. Weave over and under yourself in a scarlet ecstasy. It is all red now he comes to die. Red, with the white sparkles of those cursed stars.

Carry him gently down, and let no man know that it is the Admiral who has fallen. He covers his face and his stars with his handkerchief. The white glitter is quenched; the white glitter of his life will shine no more. "Doctor, I am gone. I leave Lady Hamilton and my daughter Horatia as a legacy to my Country." Pathetic trust, thrusting aside knowledge. Flint, the men who sit in Parliament, flint which no knocking can spark to fire. But you still believe in men's goodness, knowing only your own heart. "Let my dear Lady Hamilton have my hair, and all other things belonging to me."

The red darkens, and is filled with tossing fires. He sees Vesuvius, and over it the single silver brilliance of a star.

"One would like to live a little longer, but thank God, I have done my duty."

Slower, slower, passes the red thread and stops. The weaving is done.

In the log-book of the *Victory,* it is written: "Partial firing continued until 4.30, when a victory having been reported to the Right Honourable Lord Viscount Nelson, K.B., he died of his wound."

## CALAIS

It is a timber-yard, pungent with the smell of wood: oak, pine, and cedar. But under the piles of white boards, they say there are bones rotting. An old guide to Calais speaks of a wooden marker shaped like a battledoor, handle downwards, on the broad part of which was scratched: "Emma Hamilton, England's Friend." It was a poor thing and now even that has gone. Let us buy an oak chip for remembrance. It will only cost a sou.

*North American Review,* April 1917

# FROM GUNS AS KEYS: AND THE GREAT GATE SWINGS

## PART I

Due East, far West. Distant as the nests of the opposite winds. Removed as fire and water are, as the clouds and the roots of the hills, as the wills of youth and age. Let the key-guns be mounted, make a brave show of waging war, and pry off the lid of Pandora's box once more. Get in at any cost and let out a little, so it seems, but wait—wait—there is much to follow through the Great Gate!

They do not see things in quite that way, on this bright November day, with sun flashing, and waves splashing, up and down Chesapeake Bay. On shore, all the papers are running to press with huge headlines: "Commodore Perry Sails." Dining tables buzz with travellers' tales of old Japan culled from Dutch writers. But we are not like the Dutch. No shutting the stars and stripes up on an island. Pooh! We must trade wherever we have a mind. Naturally!

The wharves of Norfolk are falling behind, becoming smaller, confused with the warehouses and the trees. On the impetus of the strong South breeze, the paddle-wheel steam frigate, Mississippi, of the United States Navy, sails down the flashing bay. Sails away, and steams away, for her furnaces are burning, and her paddle-wheels turning, and all her sails are set and full. Pull, men, to the old chorus:

"A Yankee ship sails down the river,
Blow, boys, blow;
Her masts and spars they shine like silver,
Blow, my bully boys, blow."

But what is the use? That plaguey brass band blares out with
"The Star Spangled Banner," and you cannot hear the men be-
cause of it. Which is a pity, thinks the Commodore, in his cabin,
studying the map, and marking stepping-stones: Madeira, Cape
Town, Mauritius, Singapore, nice firm stepping-places for seven-
league boots. Flag-stones up and down a hemisphere.

My! How she throws the water off from her bows, and how
those paddle-wheels chum her along at the rate of seven good
knots! You are a proud lady, Mrs. Mississippi, curtseying down
Chesapeake Bay, all a-flutter with red white and blue ribbons.

At Mishima in the Province of Kai,
Three men are trying to measure a pine tree
By the length of their outstretched arms.
Trying to span the bole of a huge pine tree
By the spread of their lifted arms.
Attempting to compress its girth
Within the limit of their extended arms.
Beyond, Fuji,
Majestic, inevitable,
Wreathed over by wisps of cloud.
The clouds draw about the mountain,
But there are gaps.
The men reach about the pine tree,
But their hands break apart;
The rough bark escapes their hand-clasps;
The tree is unencircled.
Three men are trying to measure the stem of a gigantic pine tree,
With their arms,
At Mishima in the Province of Kai.

Furnaces are burning good Cumberland coal at the rate of
twenty-six tons per diem, and the paddlewheels turn round and

round in an iris of spray. She noses her way through a wallowing sea; foots it, bit by bit, over the slanting wave slopes; pants along, thrust forward by her breathing furnaces, urged ahead by the wind draft flattening against her taut sails.

The Commodore, leaning over the taffrail, sees the peak of Madeira swept up out of the haze. The *Mississippi* glides into smooth water, and anchors under the lee of the "Desertas."

Ah! the purple bougainvillea! And the sweet smells of the heliotrope and geranium hedges! Ox-drawn sledges clattering over cobbles—what a fine pause in an endless voyaging. Stars and stripes demanding five hundred tons of coal, ten thousand gallons of water, resting for a moment on a round steppingstone, with the drying sails slatting about in the warm wind.

"Get out your accordion, Jim, and give us the 'Sewanee River' to show those Dagos what a tune is. Pipe up with the chorus, boys. Let her go."

The green water flows past Madeira. Flows under the paddleboards, making them clip and clap. The green water washes along the sides of the Commodore's steam flagship and passes away to leeward.

"Hitch up your trousers, Black Face, and do a horn-pipe. It's a fine quiet night for a double shuffle. Keep her going, Jim. Louder. That's the ticket. Gosh, but you can spin, Blackey!"

The road is hilly
Outside the Tiger Gate,
And striped with shadows from a bow moon
Slowly sinking to the horizon.
The roadway twinkles with the bobbing of paper lanterns,
Melon-shaped, round, oblong,
Lighting the steps of those who pass along it;
And there is a sweet singing of many *semi*,
From the cages which an insect-seller
Carries on his back.

Westward of the Canaries, in a wind-blazing sea. Engineers, there, extinguish the furnaces; carpenters, quick, your screwdrivers and mallets, and unship the paddle-boards. Break out her sails, quartermasters, the wind will carry her faster than she can steam, for the trades have her now, and are whipping her along in fine clipper style. Key-guns, your muzzles shine like basalt above the tumbling waves. Polished basalt cameoed upon malachite. Yankee-doodle-dandy! A fine upstanding ship, clouded with canvas, slipping along—like a trotting filly out of the Commodore's own stables. White sails and sailors, blue-coated officers, and red in a star sparked through the claret decanter on the Commodore's luncheon table.

The Commodore is writing to his wife, to be posted at the next stopping place. Two years is a long time to be upon the sea.

Nigi-oi of Matsuba-ya
Celebrated oiran,
Courtesan of unrivalled beauty,
The great silk mercer, Mitsui,
Counts himself a fortunate man
As he watches her parade in front of him
In her robes of glazed blue silk
Embroidered with singing nightingales.
He puffs his little silver pipe
And arranges a fold of her dress.
He parts it at the neck
And laughs when the falling plum-blossoms
Tickle her naked breasts.
The next morning he makes out a bill
To the Director of the Dutch Factory at Nagasaki
For three times the amount of the goods
Forwarded that day in two small junks
In the care of a trusted clerk.

The North-east trades have smoothed away into hot, blue doldrums. Paddle-wheels to the rescue. Thank God, we live in an age of invention. What air there is, is dead ahead. The deck is a bed of cinders, we wear a smoke cloud like a funeral plume. Funeral—of whom? Of the little heathens inside the Gate? Wait! Wait! These monkey-men have got to trade, Uncle Sam has laid his plans with care, see those black guns sizzling there. "It's deuced hot," says a lieutenant, "I wish I could look in at a hop in Newport this evening."

The one hundred and sixty streets in the Sanno quarter
Are honey-gold
Honey-gold from the gold-foil screens in the houses,
Honey-gold from the fresh yellow mats;
The lintels are draped with bright colors,
And from eaves and poles
Red and white paper lanterns
Glitter and swing.
Through the one hundred and sixty decorated streets of the
    Sanno quarter,
Trails the procession,
With a bright slowness,
To the music of flutes and drums.
Great white sails of cotton
Belly out along the honey-gold streets.
Sword bearers,
Spear bearers,
Mask bearers,
Grinning masks of mountain genii,
And a white cock on a drum
Above a purple sheet.
Over the flower hats of the people,
Shines the sacred palanquin,
"Car of gentle motion,"
Upheld by fifty men,
Stalwart servants of the god,
Bending under the weight of mirror-black lacquer,
Of pillars and roof-tree
Wrapped in chased and gilded copper.
Portly silk tassels sway to the marching of feet,
Wreaths of gold and silver flowers
Shoot sudden scintillations at the gold-foil screens.

The golden phoenix on the roof of the palanquin
Spreads its wings,
And seems about to take flight
Over the one hundred and sixty streets
Straight into the white heart
Of the curved blue sky.
Six black oxen,
With white and red trappings,
Draw platforms on which are musicians, dancers, and actors,
Who posture and sing,
Dance and parade,
Up and down the honey-gold streets,
To the sweet playing of flutes,
And the ever-repeating beat of heavy drums,
To the constant banging of heavily beaten drums,
To the insistent repeating rhythm of beautiful great drums.

Across the equator and panting down to Saint Helena, trailing
smoke like a mourning veil. Jamestown jetty, and all the officers
in the ship making at once for Longwood. Napoleon! Ah, tales—
tales—with nobody to tell them. A bronze eagle caged by floating
wood-work. A heart burst with beating on a flat drop-curtain of sea
and sky. Nothing now but pigs in a sty. Pigs rooting in the Emper-
or's bedroom. God be praised, we have a plumed smoking ship to
take us away from this desolation.

"Boney was a warrior
    Away-i-oh;
Boney was a warrior,
    John François."

"Oh, shut up, Jack, you make me sick. Those pigs are like
worms eating a corpse. Bah!"

The ladies,
Wistaria Blossom, Cloth-of-Silk, and Deep Snow,
With their ten attendants,
Are come to Asakusa

To gaze at peonies.
To admire crimson-carmine peonies,
To stare in admiration at bomb-shaped, white and sulphur
   peonies,
To caress with a soft finger
Single, rose-flat peonies,
Tight, incurved, red-edged peonies,
Spin-wheel circle, amaranth peonies.
To smell the acrid pungence of peony blooms,
And dream for months afterwards
Of the temple garden at Asakusa,
Where they walked together
Looking at peonies.

The Gate! The Gate! The far-shining Gate! Pat your guns and
thank your stars you have not come too late. The Orient's a sleepy
place, as all globe-trotters say. We'll get there soon enough, my
lads, and carry it away. That's a good enough song to round the
Cape with, and there's the Table Cloth on Table Mountain and
we've drawn a bead over half the curving world. Three cheers for
Old Glory, fellows.

A Daimio's procession
Winds between two green bills,
A line of thin, sharp, shining, pointed spears
Above red coats
And yellow mushroom hats.
A man leading an ox
Has cast himself upon the ground,
He rubs his forehead in the dust,
While his ox gazes with wide, moon eyes
At the glittering spears
Majestically parading
Between two green hills.

Down, down, down, to the bottom of the map; but we must up
again, high on the other side. America, sailing the seas of a planet
to stock the shop counters at home. Commerce-raiding a nation;

pulling apart the curtains of a temple and calling it trade. Magnificent mission! Every shop-till in every by-street will bless you. Force the shut gate with the muzzles of your black cannon. Then wait—wait for fifty years—and see who has conquered.

But now the *Mississippi* must brave the Cape, in a crashing of bitter seas. The wind blows East, the wind blows West, there is no rest under these clashing clouds. Petrel whirl by like torn newspapers along a street. Albatrosses fly close to the mastheads. Dread purrs over this stormy ocean, and the smell of the water is the dead, oozing dampness of tombs.

> Tiger rain on the temple bridge of carved greenstone,
> Slanting tiger lines of rain on the lichened lanterns of the
>     gateway,
> On the stone statues of mythical warriors.
> Striped rain making the bells of the pagoda roofs flutter,
> Tiger-footing on the bluish stones of the courtyard,
> Beating, snapping, on the cheese-rounds of open umbrellas,
> Licking, tiger-tongued, over the straw mat which a pilgrim wears
>     upon his shoulders,
> Gnawing, tiger-toothed, into the paper mask
> Which he carries on his back.
> Tiger-clawed rain scattering the peach-blossoms,
> Tiger tails of rain lashing furiously among the cryptomerias.
> [ . . . ]

*Seven Arts,* August 1917

# NOTES TO THE POEMS

PART I: TRADITIONAL FORMS AND VARIATIONS
*Sonnets, Rhymed Stanzas, and Blank Verse*

ON CARPACCIO'S PICTURE: THE DREAM OF ST. URSULA
*The Dream of St. Ursula* is a tempera painting (1495) by the Venetian Vittore Carpaccio (1472–1526), in which an angel comes to the sleeping Ursula and tells her of her imminent martyrdom. The painting features an exquisitely detailed bedroom, reminiscent of Jan Vermeer's interiors, with a large double bed in which Ursula is portrayed sleeping; an angel stands at the foot of the bed. The painting, now in the Gallerie dell'Accademia in Venice, was a favorite of the Victorian art critic John Ruskin, and through him became well known.

ELEONORA DUSE
Eleonora Duse (1858–1924), the Italian actress and an inspiration for Lowell, died just before the poem was published.

AFTER WRITING "THE BRONZE HORSES"
"The Bronze Horses" appeared as the last poem in *Can Grande's Castle* and received a great deal of critical attention. The ambitious long poem describes the creation of four great horses of gilded bronze and their vicissitudes as the spoils of four wars from Rome to Constantinople to Venice.

GAVOTTE IN D MINOR
King Minos of Crete loved Dyctynna who, running away from him, leapt from a cliff into the sea to her death or, as it is told in some versions, was caught in a fisherman's net and rescued by Artemis.

SONG FOR A VIOLA D'AMORE
A viola d'amore is a viol with numerous sympathetic strings and several gut strings that produces a deeply resonant sound.

The most beautiful of men, Endymion was loved by Selēne, or Diana (the Moon). He was thrown into a perpetual sleep and was visited each night by her.

### On Looking at a Copy of Alice Meynell's Poems, Given Me, Years Ago, by a Friend

Alice Meynell (1847–1922), a popular and prolific British journalist as well as a poet, published her *Collected Poems* in 1913 to such strong praise that she was mentioned as a candidate for poet laureateship. In 1897, while Lowell was recovering from a serious illness, Frances Dabney, a good friend, gave her a volume of Meynell's poems.

### The Sisters

This poem manipulates blank verse, similar to practices of Lowell's contemporaries, Robert Frost and Wallace Stevens; Lowell also alludes to blank verse manipulations by Elizabeth Barrett Browning and Robert Browning.

The original published version has the line "Strange trio of my sisters, most diverse" as the end of the verse paragraph, whereas in the final version this line begins the next paragraph. Because of the punctuation (a semicolon), the next line beginning with "And," and the sense of the paragraph, we have accepted the final version of the poem and include it here.

## Adapted Asian Forms and Translations from the Chinese

### One of the "Hundred Views of Fuji" by Hokusai

Because Hokusai (1760–1849) studied Western art, he is not typical of most Japanese artists. His most famous series of woodcuts is *Thirty-six Views of Fuji* (1829–33), the best known of which is *The Great Wave.*

### Li T'ai-po

Li T'ai-po (701–762), one of the most popular poets during the T'ang dynasty, is known for the spontaneity and vividness of his lyrics. He remains one of the great poets of world literature and a supreme celebrator of pleasure and loss. It is no wonder, therefore, that Amy Lowell found in his poetry a soul mate.

### Nostalgia

The opening line is an adaptation of the first line of a song, "Home! Sweet Home!" (1823; words by John Howard Paine [1791–1852] and music by Henry Rowley Bishop [1791–1855]), partly taken from a Sicilian air. The original lyrics read, "'Mid pleasures and palaces though we may roam / Be it ever so humble / There's no place like home."

## THE RETREAT OF HSIEH KUNG

Hsieh Kung is the honorary title of Hsieh T'iao, a poet esteemed by Li T'ai-po.

## IN THE PROVINCE OF LU, TO THE EAST OF THE STONE GATE MOUNTAIN, TAKING LEAVE OF TU FU

Tu Fu (712–770), with Li T'ai-po and Wang Wei considered among the greats of Chinese poetry, spent many years as a poor wanderer. Unlike the pleasure-loving Li T'ai-po, he wrote about sufferings of the poor and about corruption, but with an ironic humor and hope. Known as a scholar's poet, his auto-biography was translated by Lowell's collaborator, the sinologist Florence Ayscough.

## THE BLUE-GREEN STREAM

The third of the great Tang dynasty poets, Wang Wei (699–761) continued the tradition of the poetry of retreat while also serving in the Tang court. The ideas of retreat, a combination of Taoism, Buddhism, and Confucianism, in-cluded the notion of community while living away from society in order to cultivate personal values.

## PART II: CADENCED VERSE

### AUBADE

An *aubade* (also *alba*) is a dawn song of no fixed metrical form, usually ex-pressing two lovers' regret at the coming of the day that necessitates their parting.

### THE TAXI

"I call out for you against the jutted stars": in deference to Lowell's final ver-sion of the poem, we have removed the period from the end of this line as it first appeared in *The Egoist*.

### PINE, BEECH, AND SUNLIGHT

This was included in *Pictures of the Floating World* as "Beech, Pine, and Sun-light," a title that better corresponds to the sequence in the poem.

### VENUS TRANSIENS

The Sandro Botticelli (1445–1510) work *The Birth of Venus* (c. 1483), now in the Ufizzi Gallery in Florence, has been venerated from its inception to the present. It represents a willowy figure standing on a scallop shell, being wafted ashore by waves and the wind, which also spreads her hair in a fan around her head.

## WAKEFULNESS

The Battersea Bridge spans the Thames River in London at Cheyne Walk, in the neighborhood of Chelsea. The bridge is a subject of a painting by James McNeill Whistler, *Nocturne: Blue and Gold— Old Battersea Bridge,* described similarly in this poem.

## A BATHER

"After a Picture by Andreas Zorn" is the subtitle added in the volume *Pictures of the Floating World,* indicating an ecphrastic poem, a poem describing a work of art.

## THE BROKEN FOUNTAIN

The original publication, handmade and distributed locally from Wellesley, Massachusetts, had "paleness" for the stronger "pale uncertainty" from *Pictures of the Floating World.* We reprint Lowell's correction here.

## THE WEATHERVANE POINTS SOUTH

This was published as "The Weather-Cock Points South" in *Pictures of the Floating World.*

## SEPTEMBER. 1918

September 1918 was a time of major Allied offensives during World War I.

## GRANADILLA

"And yet I come back to it again and again": in the version of this poem published in *Coterie* there was a comma at the end of this line; we have replaced it with the period that Lowell used in the later, collected version.

## ON READING A LINE UNDERSCORED BY KEATS

*Palmerin of England,* a chivalric romance of uncertain authorship, is referred to in *Don Quixote.* Lowell examined the copy John Keats borrowed from his friend John Taylor and, according to Lowell in her biography of Keats, "filled it with appreciative scorings."

## DISSONANCE

The Pre-Raphaelites were a group of British Victorian writers and artists that included the painters Edward Colley Burne-Jones, Arthur Hughes, William Holman Hunt, John Everett Millais, and Dante Gabriel Rossetti. Organized in 1848 as the Pre-Raphaelite Brotherhood, they resolved to be inspired by painters before Raphael, indicating their rebellion against the academic paintings of their day, which they dismissed as "slosh." Landscape painting was not their specialty.

Lowell may be referring here to James McNeill Whistler, whose paintings of the Thames River in London could be described as "lightly touched with ebony and silver," colors not usually found in the Pre-Raphaelite palette.

PART III: POLYPHONIC PROSE

SPRING DAY

BREAKFAST TABLE

A Catherine wheel is a kind of firework, named for St. Catherine's martyrdom, that is ignited and revolves on a pin, making a wheel of fire.

FROM MALMAISON

Malmaison, the chateau purchased by Josephine Bonaparte in 1799, together with the Tuileries, was the French government's headquarters from 1800 to 1802. When Napoleon Bonaparte moved to Saint-Cloud, Josephine stayed in Malmaison and commissioned a wide range of improvements. She settled in permanently after her divorce in 1809 and died there on May 29, 1814.

FROM SEA-BLUE AND BLOOD-RED

The poem dramatizes the love affair of Admiral Horatio Nelson (1758–1805), the greatest British hero of his time, and Emma, Lady Hamilton (1765–1815), renowned beauty and wife of the much older William, Lord Hamilton (1730–1803), from the Battle of the Nile and their first meeting to Nelson's death during the Battle of Trafalgar and her death, in poverty and neglect, ten years later in Calais.

In the "Calais" section of the version of this poem that was printed in the *North American Review,* "oak" was capitalized; for consistency's sake here we have removed the capital letter.

# INDEX OF TITLES

# INDEX OF FIRST LINES

# ABOUT THE EDITORS

Melissa Bradshaw is an assistant professor of interdisciplinary humanities at Barat College of DePaul University. She is currently completing a manuscript on Amy Lowell.

Adrienne Munich is a professor of English and women's studies at the State University of New York–Stony Brook. She is the author of *Queen Victoria's Secrets* and *Andromeda's Chains: Gender and Interpretation in Victorian Literature and Art* and coeditor of *Arms and the Woman* and *Remaking Queen Victoria*.